DECORATE WITH

Quilts & Collections

DECORATE WITH
Quilts & Collections

Nancy J. Martin

That Patchwork Place

Acknowledgments

To all the homeowners, who graciously allowed us to photograph their lovely homes.

To the quilt collectors, who generously shared their collections.

To Brent Kane, whose continual artistry with the camera contributes so much to my work.

To the staff of That Patchwork Place, Inc., especially Marta Estes and Cindy Knutzen, whose support and encouragement are appreciated.

To Sharon and Jason Yenter of In The Beginning Fabrics, for information on home-decorating fabrics.

To Jean Coulbourne of Everfast Fabrics, for technical information.

To the Ritter Cabinet Company, for providing even more sewing cabinets.

To Cleo Nollette, Kristin Jarvis, Suzanne Nelson, and Laurie Bevan, whose nimble fingers stitched to meet decorating deadlines.

To Alvina Nelson (Star of Provence), Lea Wang (Medallion), and Amanda Miller's quilters (Shaded Nine Patch), for their fine quilting.

To Joan Hanson, who was always there with her home-economics background and the right answer.

To Deanna Heathcock, for stitching the slipcovers for the living room of our Woodinville home.

To Mary Terry of Esther's Fabrics on Bainbridge Island, for stitching the slipcovers for the beach house.

To Retta Warehime, Terry Guizzo, and Barb Ward, for their encouragement and readiness to share new ideas.

To Cherry Jarvis, whose enthusiasm for new decorating projects with a high cuteness factor helps keep me going.

To Alice Berg, who encouraged me to design fabric.

To David Peha of FASCO, who provided me with the opportunity to design the Room Mates™ line of fabrics.

To Dan Martin, without whose technical support and open checkbook this project would not have been possible.

Credits

Editor-in-Chief .... Kerry I. Hoffman
Managing Editor .... Judy Petry
Technical Editor .... Sharon Rose
Copy Editor ....Liz McGehee
Proofreader .... Melissa Riesland
Illustrator ....Laurel Strand
Photographer .... Brent Kane
Text and Cover Designer .... Barbara Schmitt
Production Assistants .... Shean Bemis,
Mona Evans, Marijane Figg,
Claudia L'Heureux, Marge Mueller

Dedication

To my first grandchild, Megan Jane Martin. May you find the joy derived by creating new and exciting home-decorating settings and replacing them often. Learn to love fabric and let it brighten your life and the rooms of those you love.

Decorate with Quilts and Collections
© 1996 by Nancy J. Martin
That Patchwork Place, Inc.
PO Box 118
Bothell, WA 98041-0118 USA

Printed in Hong Kong
01 00 99 98 97 96   6 5 4 3 2 1

Library of Congress Cataloging-in-Publication Data
Martin, Nancy J.
  Decorate with quilts and collections / by Nancy J. Martin.
     p.   cm.
  ISBN 1-56477-158-X
  1. Quilts.   2. Patchwork—Patterns.   3. Quilts in interior decoration.   4. Americana in interior decoration.   I. Title.
TT835.M2733 1996
747'.9—dc20   96-22451
                                                                              CIP

Contents

Introduction

Quilts are an integral part of decorating schemes in many home interiors. From Victorian to contemporary, from New England to Southern California, quilts make an appearance on walls and beds, over cupboard doors, and stacked on shelves. As I researched this sequel to *Make Room for Quilts,* I was amazed at the similarities in the homes of quilters and quilt collectors. But even more amazing than the similarities are the different creative solutions to common decorating problems.

Color and fabric are two of the most versatile media for enhancing and changing decorating schemes. The homeowners in this book change their interior decors often for that very reason. Quilts punctuate these rooms, making a bold graphic statement or adding a soft nostalgic touch. Many of the rooms echo the quilts with stenciling or decorative painting.

Though the primary intent of *Decorate with Quilts and Collections* is to once again inspire you with stunning photographs of well-decorated homes, I have also sought new ways to present helpful decorating ideas and information. Throughout the book, you'll find special highlighted sections called "Decorator Touches." Each is designed to give you additional information, including diagrams and photos, on a specific decorating idea.

While visiting the homes showcased in this book, I couldn't help noticing the abundance of collections often sharing center stage with the quilts. Focusing on these collections expanded the theme of this volume and allowed me to include rooms more appropriate for collections than for quilts, such as kitchens and bathrooms.

Part I features tours of more than a dozen homes chosen to inspire and delight you, each abundant with quilts and collections. Large and small, some owned by popular designers and artists within the quilt world, the homes reflect the personalities and individual styles of their owners.

In Part II, we visit the homes of four prominent quilt collectors to see how they display, store, and live with their treasures. Part III provides an in-depth look at various rooms. I hope it will give you some fresh ideas for decorating your home, including creative ways to display collections.

In the final section of the book, helpful information is given on selecting colors and fabrics for home decor. Step-by-step directions are provided for twenty-five easy projects, including bed skirts, window treatments, pillows, and three bed-size quilts.

Providing a cozy and inviting home for family and friends is the goal of many homeowners. The warmth and comfort emanating from treasured quilts knows no equal. As you seek inspiration among the pages of this book, remember, "A quilt is a blanket of love."

Opposite page: Sofas upholstered in beige-and-white ticking hold a scrappy quilt and pillows made from old quilt blocks. A red-and-white checked rug highlights the seating area where a child's picnic table serves as a coffee table.

Child's Play

On a quiet, tree-lined street in Marietta, Georgia, an unassuming yellow frame house gives little clue to the exuberant setting that lies therein. Home to Alice and Wally Berg, the house is filled with myriad quilts and collections that are displayed with layers of style and southern charm. Alice is a quilter and one-third of a trio of talented quilt designers known as Little Quilts. Wally is an insurance executive who enjoys golf, woodworking, and carving small birds for Alice to incorporate in her decorating schemes.

And what schemes they are! Alice collects patriotic memorabilia, folk art, bears, children's toys, vintage textiles, doll dresses, and, of course, Little Quilts. The vignettes she arranges throughout her home are just as appealing as those she does for Little Quilts pattern covers. Fun, whimsy, and splashes of color appear in just the right amounts. In addition to quilting, Alice loves rug hooking. She hooked most of the small rugs, pillows, and wall hangings in her home.

Above: Bears from the North American Bear Company® (there is one in every Little Quilts photo) rest on a church pew, surrounded by Alice's collection of children's toys. Alice hooked the Three Bears rug with her three sons in mind.

Right: Hooked rugs, a Little Quilt, and a shelf full of miniatures are displayed on the back wall.

Right: A Tree of Life medallion quilt, typical of those Alice enjoys designing and making, is displayed on the wall behind a pie safe with tin-punched doors.

Below: A framed antique Feathered Star quilt block hangs above the mantel. A painted green watering can and a chair holding an appliquéd Laurel Leaf pillow add splashes of color.

Below: A grouping of patriotic memorabilia collected by Alice

Above: A Schoolhouse quilt from Little Quilts
shares the wall with an old slate, a class picture,
Amish dresses, and other collectibles.

Right: A jelly cabinet with tin-punched doors hides a
collection of Pfaltzgraff® pottery. A Bear Paw quilt from
Little Quilts drapes over the top of the cabinet, and a
Crazy quilt embroidered with initials hangs over the door.

Alice's quilt "Homecoming" (right) won the *Better Homes and Gardens* 1993 quilt contest. It hangs in her dining room above a collection of folk art, including work by Howard Fenzer.

The master suite is decorated in red, white, and blue and highlighted with patriotic accents. Here, an Eagle quilt perches under the eaves.

Right: An antique Nine Patch quilt hangs over the bed next to a patriotic rug hooked by Alice.

Hooked on Folk Art

Built in the early 1900s as a summer retreat, this group of frame structures lies on the Chattahoochee River in Roswell, Georgia. Owners Susan and Roger Morin have lovingly restored and renovated the main house, guest house, and barn.

Susan, a collector of folk art, quilts, and textiles, has carefully worked her collections into the home's decor. She is also an accomplished rug hooker and a certified McGown teacher. Roger, a professor of finance at Georgia State University, enjoys carpentry and woodworking. He has skillfully restored many of their antique treasures, including some found in his native Nova Scotia.

The Morins' renovation improved the room layout and raised the ceilings to the roof line. To provide structural strength for the roof, bands of black iron span the interior ceiling, with adjustable tension bars at each end. The contractor visits the house at regular intervals to tune the iron bands and adjust the tension, keeping the roof properly aligned. Curved archways link the rooms and repeat the rounded elements used in both the house and guest house. Large windows with a view of the river — along with natural materials, such as wood and ceramic tile — link the house to its natural setting.

Opposite page:
The sunroom stretches across the back of the house, offering views of the Chattahoochee River from its many windows. Filled with comfortable furniture, antiques, and hooked rugs, the room invites relaxation.

Right: An antique bench, once used for nursing babies, holds an assortment of pillows and folk-art dolls. The Noah's Ark rug was hooked by Susan.

Folk-art collectibles are grouped on top of this antique apothecary chest.

Left: Susan made this penny rug to fit the round table.

A Log Cabin quilt stitched in warm colors hangs over the sofa, where a Basket quilt covers the seat cushions. A bright Tumbling Blocks quilt decorates the table in the dining alcove.

Below: An antique Signature quilt hangs high above the kitchen cabinets between two tall windows.

Right: A collectible Noah's Ark is arranged on top of an antique oak cupboard from Nova Scotia.

Left: Kitchen collectibles and a checkerboard made by Roger's grandfather hang on the wall above a shelf full of quilts.

Below: A bright Log Cabin quilt top is draped over a stool near the kitchen island. An oak corner cupboard holds kitchen pottery.

In Roger's guesthouse office, double doors open to a view of the river. Alice Berg made "Election Year," the quilt on the desk.

Right: Antique quilts and quilt tops cover and surround a twin bed in the loft of the guest house. Quilts hung over the railing block the view from below and add an element of coziness.

Below: In another guest room, an antique tied patchwork comforter serves as the backdrop for a rope bed spread with a Christmas sampler quilt.

Left: In a loft bedroom in the guest house, an iron bed echoes the window's curves. A geometric Tumbling Blocks quilt and striped and checked pillowcases offer the perfect counterpoint.

Below: A miniature Dresden Plate quilt protects the bedside table.

In Our Nation's Capital

*T*his contemporary house on an urban street in Washington, D.C., is home to quiltmaker Lee Porter and her businessman husband, Robert. The house was built in 1978 by architect-builder Win Faulkner. Its three stories are linked by both stairs and an elevator.

Lee is a seminary student and fabric artist who makes original pictorial quilts, often on Biblical themes. These pictorial quilts hang on the walls, and her earlier block-style and antique quilts cover the beds. Lee has collected quilts for a number of years and has many scrap-bag quilts, as well as examples of other styles.

Lee's work has been featured in several exhibitions and has sold well. A former quilt-shop owner, she occasionally teaches and lectures on quiltmaking. She also enjoys stenciling and has used this medium in her home, including the wood floors and an original design in the elevator.

Opposite page: Lee stenciled the wood floor in the first-floor dining room in a classic geometric pattern. A textile table runner and quilts hung on the wall and draped over a chair soften the room.

In the third floor hallway, an embroidered fund-raising quilt is mounted on stretcher bars. A Crazy quilt is draped over the stairwell, and Lee's "Biblical Jubilee" graces the back wall.

Decorator Touches

Stenciled Wood Floors

Materials

Graph paper
Large sheet of Mylar® for stencil
X-Acto® knife
¼"-wide masking tape
Stencil paint
Sponge
Varathane® varnish and brush

Stencil pattern for floor

Border detail of stenciled floor shown on page 27

Directions

1. Use graph paper to draw a diagram of the room. Allowing space for a stenciled border, divide the remaining area into equal-size squares. Choose a size that divides evenly into the length and width of the area.

2. Cut the Mylar 4" larger than the squares on the diagram. Example: 16" x 16" for 12" squares.

3. Transfer your design onto the Mylar with a pencil. Cut out the stencil using the X-Acto knife.

4. Prepare the floor for stenciling. Remove the old finish and carefully sand the floor. Make sure it is smooth and free of all dust and debris. With the masking tape, mark the floor into squares as indicated on the diagram.

5. Align the Mylar stencil with a marked square on the floor.

6. Following the manufacturer's directions, apply stencil paint with a sponge. Let dry.

7. Repeat steps 2–6 for the border.

8. Following the manufacturer's directions, apply 2 coats of varnish.

In the second-floor living room, a turn-of-the-century quilt top is folded over the sofa back. Lee's pictorial quilt "Blessed Is the Man Whose Faith Is Like a Tree" is on the far wall.

Below: Detail of the antique quilt top and assorted pillows

Left: An antique Rosebud quilt from Oklahoma rests on a chair.

Right: An upstairs bedroom holds some of Lee's early quilts: "Mistake" and an Oak Leaf quilt done in Laura Ashley fabrics. An old oak cabinet stores more quilts from her collection.

Below: The cozy master bedroom is warmed by earth tones, stacks of books, family photos, and a Log Cabin quilt made by Lee on the bed. A red-and-white antique quilt is folded over the chair.

Right: Lee houses part of her quilt collection, including this graphic zigzag Log Cabin, in her study.

Decorator Touches

Quilt Rack

Materials

Two lengths of 2" x 4" lumber, each long
enough to reach from floor to ceiling
Wooden dowels, 2" in diameter and long
enough to span the desired width
(number depends on ceiling height)
Varathane® varnish and brush

Directions

1. Draw notches spaced 10" apart on each
   2" x 4".
2. Using a hole saw, drill a hole ¼" to ½"
   larger than the dowel. Place the hole ¼"
   to ½" from the "back" edge of the wood.
3. Cut a notch at an angle, from the "front"
   edge of the wood to the hole.

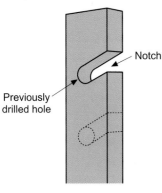

Notch

Previously
drilled hole

4. Using long wood screws, mount the 2" x
   4" boards to wall studs, placing screws
   inside every other notch. Paint to match
   the walls.
5. Varnish the dowels. When dry, insert into
   the notches.

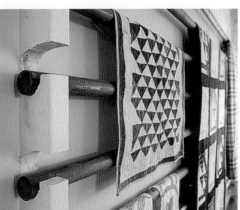

Above: Lee fashioned a unique rack for displaying
quilts and other textiles. Hanging on the rack are a
red-and-white doll quilt, appliqué pieces, an antique
Basket quilt, and blue-and-white–plaid mattress
ticking. At the foot of the bed is a boudoir quilt from
Robert's family. This quilt is thought to have been
made in Oklahoma City during the 1930s or '40s.

Left: Detail of support that holds wood dowels

An Old-Fashioned Girl

Nestled among blooming trees and flower beds in a community near Yakima, Washington, is the picture-postcard house of Khay and Don Norris. This Victorian, built in 1904, has been lovingly restored by the owners, then decorated with quilts Khay has either made or collected. The charming interiors serve as the perfect backdrop for Khay's china, toys, and Tartan collectibles.

Khay manages the gift shop at the Yakima Valley Museum and stitches with a group of local quilters. She enjoys making miniature quilts, which lend themselves to display in her vintage home. An accomplished needlewoman, Khay also enjoys embroidery, rug hooking, and dollmaking.

Khay challenged herself to work with the small rooms and the colors and fixtures already present in the interiors. The most challenging of these were the apple green walls in the living and dining rooms. The large Victorian bathroom, located in the center of the first floor, is a focal point between the downstairs rooms.

Opposite page: **The apple green walls in the dining room are softened by the white ceiling molding, window trim, and large corner cupboard.**

Right: Pink-and-white transferware plates are arranged on the wall above the sideboard. The plate and wall colors complement the pink-and-green Bear's Paw quilt spread on the table. Crocheted doilies slip over the chair backs.

Below: A bookshelf in the dining room holds several of Khay's miniature quilts.

Right: An assortment of china fills the shelves above a group of collectible boxes stacked on an antique penny rug.

Below: The pink-and-green color scheme continues across the hall in the living room. A Garden Twist quilt top made by Khay drapes over the sofa back, and a Yo-yo quilt covers the table by the window.

Above: The tiny master bedroom features an assortment of quilts. A Double Wedding Ring quilt is on the bed with a pink Bow Tie quilt folded at the foot. Additional Bow Tie quilts are on the wall and over the chair back.

Right: New and old pillows, adorned with turkey-work embroidery, grace the head of the bed. More turkey work, done by Khay, is framed and hung on the sprigged wall paper. The sheer curtains and bed canopy filter delicate light into the room.

The downstairs Victorian bathroom is large enough to fill with an assortment of treasures. Small quilts nestle among shelves of china. Large folded quilts share space with vintage textiles. Flowered hats from days gone by are right at home with the floral accents in this crisp pink-and-white color scheme.

Right: A simple Nine Patch quilt and a Basket quilt are moved outdoors for entertaining on special occasions.

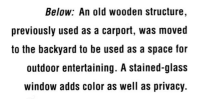

Below: An old wooden structure, previously used as a carport, was moved to the backyard to be used as a space for outdoor entertaining. A stained-glass window adds color as well as privacy.

Southern Hospitality

*K*arin and Charlie Snyder live in a saltbox home on a quiet street in Marietta, Georgia. Karin, a former antiques dealer who now works in the office of Little Quilts, has filled the home with southern primitive antiques, quilts, and collections. The Snyders have remodeled several times, adding generously proportioned rooms that accommodate larger pieces of furniture. Quilts include a mixture of homey, full-size quilts and smaller pieces made from Little Quilts designs.

The home's interior is full of Karin's collections, yet the high ceilings, transom windows, white wainscoting, and light floors combine to create a feeling of spaciousness. From the iron stars, which are architectural embellishments, to the tin ice box on the deck, pieces of the past are given both decorative and functional uses.

Opposite page: Homey, scrappy quilts hang on the wall and over the backs of chairs, while smaller pieces, cut from worn or damaged quilts, are used as antimacassars on the sofas.

Above: Iron stars that once embellished steel rods on old buildings now decorate the corners of the eating area. A collection of wooden rolling pins is stacked in an antique dough bowl. The table runner was cut from a badly damaged quilt.

Right: A hooked House pillow from a Little Quilts pattern perches atop a group of antique benches. Shuttered doors leading to the deck make it easy to control light.

"Welcome," a Little Quilts design, graces the dining room table.

The rich, warm tones of pine furniture in the dining room complement the flow-blue china in the hutch.

Right: A cheery antique Bear's Paw quilt hangs in the foyer above an old slant-top desk. A peg rail of patriotic items decorates the hallway.

Left: Taupe-and-white–striped wallpaper in the hall and stairway creates a cool, crisp backdrop for collectibles, including antique crocks.

Left: A teddy bear collection sits beneath a Bow Tie quilt made from a Little Quilts design.

Below: Taupe-and-white–checked wallpaper is a neutral backdrop for antique quilts and Americana collectibles. The muted, scrappy quilts on the curved iron beds are brightened by the red-and-white quilts folded at the footboards: an Ocean Waves quilt on the left and a Double T on the right. An antique sewing-machine cabinet serves as a bedside table.

Above: Fresh flowers and a scrappy quilt brighten this corner of the room.

Right: Antique quilts, carefully folded and arranged, warm the back of this wicker sofa.

A new addition at the rear of the house is lightened by transom windows and French doors leading to a deck. Shutters on both the windows and doors control light. The antique wicker furniture was painted at a car-painting facility. Upholstered cushions in stars and stripes add sparkle to the room.

Right: A scrappy quilt hangs above an old grain bin. Another quilt, a Magic Carpet design, is folded over the chaise longue.

Below: An antique Triangles quilt whose bright colors echo those of the pool balls fills a wide expanse between two windows. Karin purchased the stained-glass windows from a church about to be renovated.

Left: An old cooler that once held bottles of cold pop is now used to serve drinks on the deck. A House quilt, made from a Little Quilts pattern, rests on the chaise.

Below: A watermelon pillow and an antique Le Moyne Star quilt are moved out to the deck for a punch of color when the Snyders entertain.

49

Homespun Happiness

Linda and Robert Brannock's home in Independence, Missouri, is a tribute to their combined talents and hard work. Linda, a fabric artist, markets her patterns and books under the Star Quilt Co. label. Robert, an airline supervisor, is a talented woodworker who has crafted much of the furniture and many of the display pieces found in their home. Linda is a bundle of energy and ideas. Her creative touch is evident throughout the house and in the wonderful backyard garden they have created.

Linda has been collecting for more than twenty years and is a master at arranging her collections and integrating them into the room's decor, often using them to disguise functional or unattractive items. Linda has had a profound influence on quiltmakers and collectors, first as a member of the design team at Red Wagon Originals, then with her own Star Quilt Co. Along with Jan Patek, she has designed a line of woven plaid fabrics called "From the Prairie."

Plaids abound in her quilts and throughout the house. Linda even stitches her bedsheets and pillowcases from brushed plaids so they will coordinate with her quilts. Subtle colors give the house a warm, mellow feel. The distinctive look of her quilts is achieved by overdyeing the fabrics with tan dye.

Linda has enjoyed many forms of needlework since she began stitching doll clothes at the tender age of six. Her talent and interest range from quiltmaking to rug hooking, from embroidery to cross-stitch.

Opposite page: The living room in the Brannock home is a treasure trove of work by friends and fellow artisans. The wide-plank wood floors, installed by John Laurof, complement the wall quilt "The Sun, the Moon, and the Stars" from Star Quilt Co. Hooked rugs by Annette Vaughn were also done for the company. The Basket quilt, which is from Linda's book *All My Best*, is draped over a television cupboard made by Robert, who also built the shelves.

The entry area is defined by a low wall and a collection of architectural stars hung near the ceiling. The quilt rack and fireside chair, both made by Robert, enhance Linda's quilts.

Decorator Touches

Primitive Curtains

Materials

44"-wide fabric (amount depends on
  window measurement)
Embroidery floss
String
Blunt needle
Small tacks

Directions

1. Measure across the inside of the window frame at the top. This number is the width of each panel. Measure down the inside of the frame, adding 1" extra for the top casing.

Note: The edges of the curtains are frayed, so you don't need to add extra for hems.

2. Cut 2 panels for each window.
3. Staystitch ½" from the side and bottom edges. Pull the threads to fray the fabric to this stitching line.
4. Fold top edge under 1". Using embroidery floss, stitch the casing along the raw edge of the fabric.
5. Cut a piece of string twice the width of the inside of the window frame.
6. Using the blunt needle, thread the string through the casings of both curtain panels. Do not trim the excess string.
7. Place a tack in the inside top corner of each window frame.
8. To hang the curtains, wrap the excess string around each tack, allowing the remainder of the string to hang down. The curtains should dip in the center.

String holds a primitive curtain above wooden shutters.

Left: Plaid curtains and Log Cabin place mats warm the eating area.

Below: Primitive collectibles are gathered on the screened porch that overlooks the lush backyard garden. Linda hooked the farm-scene rug and made the Sheriff's Star quilt; Robert made the birdhouses.

Above: A basket full of wooden watermelon slices and iron trivets, and Pfaltzgraff® pottery with a basket design decorate the table.

Right: The keeping room holds wonderful collections of pottery, quilts, and wooden ware, all softened by baskets and bunches of flowers and herbs hanging from overhead beams. The table runner is from *Red Wagon Originals*, and the Star Basket quilt is one of Linda's patterns.

Folded quilts and textiles spill out of the open shelves of this primitive cupboard.

Linda painted the headboard and fashioned the plaid bed linens. She finds that 12 yards of 60"-wide fabric will usually make one set of sheets (flat and fitted) for a queen-size bed. She used 2 yards of fabric to make the pillow, stuffed it with batting, then knotted one end.

Linda received the reproduction pencil-post bed as a thirtieth-anniversary gift from her husband. It was made by artisan Bernie Stanchek, who also crafted the wood shutters throughout the house. Spread with homemade sheets and a quilt from a Star Quilt Co. pattern, the bed invites snuggling under the covers.

Below: Linda's quilts hang on a wall rack specially made by her husband.

Above: Another stack of quilts in homespun colors warms a corner of the room.

Right: Books with wool covers, designed by Maggie Bonanomi, are grouped together on the bed.

Below: The bedcover and pillows in this room are made from fabrics designed by Linda and Jan Patek. Folded at the foot of the bed is an Easy Stars quilt from the Star Quilt Co.

Decorator Touches

Clever Camouflage

To disguise unsightly areas, out-of-date fixtures, or modern-day appliances that clash with a primitive decor, try camouflaging with antique boxes and other similarly shaped items.

1. Begin by placing the largest and heaviest item at the base.

2. Stack boxes in rows. It is not necessary for all items in the stack to be the same width. Build each stack, placing narrower and lighter items on top. Also use decorative items that have a box-like shape.

3. Include items made from a variety of materials to add textural interest.

A peg rail mounted about 10" below the ceiling draws the eye up, away from fixtures you want to de-emphasize (See photos opposite.) Here are a few tips for decorating the rail:

■ Use lots of items made from various kinds of old wood for textural interest. Also include items with distressed painted surfaces.

■ Use items with a variety of shapes.

■ Include bunches of dried herbs and wreaths for a touch of nature.

Above: A collection of wooden boxes, houses, and drying trays stacked across the back side of the kitchen counter camouflage the unsightly backs of the microwave oven (lower left corner) and other appliances.

Right: A tin-punch lamp casts irregular shadows on the ceiling, hiding imperfections. The Angel quilt is from Linda's book *All My Best*.

Wood boxes and other items draw attention away from the dated blue ceramic tile and fixtures in the bathroom.

Old wooden shutters take the place of a shower curtain on the tub. A quilt hangs from a towel rack, and more wooden boxes, holding sponges and bathroom items, are stacked in a corner.

Aromatic herb wreaths and bouquets, hung with other collectibles on a peg rail, release pleasant scents in a steamy bathroom. An old sewing-machine drawer holds washcloths.

A Prolific Quilter

Donna and David Radner live in a house lit by the vivid colors of her quilts. Donna, a fiber artist and teacher, resides with her economist husband in Chevy Chase, Maryland. She specializes in Bargello quilts, whose rhythmic patterns send bands of color dancing through the rooms of her home.

Through her design business, Impressions, Donna teaches and writes about quilting, and designs commissioned quilts. Her sewing studio, shown on pages 180–81, is packed with brightly colored fabrics, attesting to her love of vibrantly colored quilts.

Donna's love of vivid color is also evident in the dishes and pottery she collects. To showcase the intense colors of her quilts and pottery, Donna chose neutral backgrounds throughout her home: cool white walls, warm wood tones for the floors, and wicker furniture. These neutrals are the perfect foil for Donna's quilts.

Opposite page: The clear, strong pastel colors of the quilts and pillows make this back porch a welcome retreat in summer heat. Pieced by Donna and quilted by Fannie Horst, these quilts are brought out onto the porch only for special occasions. "Impressionist Garden in Early Spring" hangs on the wall, and "Watercolor Streams" accents the chair.

Above: A pastel Bargello quilt
made by Donna mimics the
colors of the chair cushions.

Left: A Birds in Flight quilt
made by Donna hangs above
a wooden bench.

Left: Striped sofas, softened by pastel print pillows, coordinate with three of Donna's quilts hanging on the living room walls.

Below: Named "Rose Garden," this Crazy Patch Log Cabin quilt hangs in the laundry room.

Both of these diagonally cut Bargello quilts are original designs
pieced by Donna and quilted by Fannie Horst. "Turbulent Waters"
hangs on the wall, while "Tropical Waters" is folded over the sofa.

Below: A pastel quilt called "Cherry Blossom Time" hangs in the dining room above the buffet.

Above: Bargello place mats and a matching table runner brighten a table set with brightly colored pottery. Donna made "Undercurrents," the intertwining Bargello quilt hanging on the wall.

A Collection of Collections

*T*he home of Christal and Bill Carter in Valley Center, California, overflows with collections. They purchased the hillside property more than twenty years ago and built a Spanish-style home overlooking the scenic countryside. Over the years, they made several additions to their home, the most recent being a large living room on the front of the house. Now that her two daughters no longer live at home, Christal has even more rooms to decorate!

A quilter for more than twenty years, Christal is a designer and author of several books published by That Patchwork Place. She also self-publishes a line of patterns and operates Majestic Seasons, a decorating service for seasonal home decor, special events, and theme parties. She brings all this talent and know-how to decorating her own home.

One of Christal's special talents is giving new life to used items found at tag sales, thrift shops, and antique stores. The nooks and crannies of Christal's house are filled with her collections. She is always on the lookout for odd pieces of furniture and display fixtures, especially pedestals. When shopping for new pieces to add to her collections, she looks for overscale or undersize items and especially for anything whimsical.

Opposite: The new living room holds a collection of small objects on the table (inset), heart-shaped boxes on the floor, and candlesticks on the mantel. The fireplace alcove repeats the shape of the arched window, and the quilt draped over the sofa back ties the rich, warm color scheme together.

A Cherry Basket quilt hangs on a rack next to an improvised hutch. The cabinet top and butcher-block bottom were found at different times in different shops. With her skillful eye, Christal saw their potential and combined them.

In an alcove high above the living room, an antique decoy and a Crazy quilt from Christal's family are surrounded by plants.

Decorator Touches

Found Furniture

Used imaginatively, antiques and vintage furniture—even functional pieces—can add a touch of whimsy, romance, or nostalgia to a room. Whether as backdrops or for storage, try integrating some of these treasures from yesteryear into your rooms.

Left: Two vintage suitcases topped by a wooden bed tray make up this unique coffee table.

A receipt from the Bank of San Bernardino was found in this old copper check-filing cabinet. Christal recycled this utilitarian piece into a striking accent for the corner of her family room.

A sale of department-store fixtures yielded an ideal piece on which to display quilts.

Leftover Log Cabin blocks are fashioned into a patchwork valance.

"Special Delivery," an original design by Christal, hangs on a quilt rack near the woodstove.

Antique quilts and new quilt tops assembled with Christal's Split Log Cabin technique share the spotlight in the family room.

More collectibles are found in the pantry along with variations of the Log Cabin quilt hanging on the wall.

A collection of Santa Claus mugs and plates fills the hutch in the breakfast room. A Christmas Wreath table runner protects the hutch, and the quilt "A Sweet Valentine" brightens the table in front of the heart-decorated tree.

A charming Santa quilt directs the viewer's attention to the collection of Santa Claus figurines, tins, and plates displayed in the cupboard.

Above: "Strawberries and Tea," an original design by Christal, is part of a Valentine display in the pantry.

Decorator Touches

Patchwork Desk Blotter

Leftover patchwork blocks were used to fashion a desk blotter for this feminine office. A Cherry Basket wall hanging adorns the back of the chair.

Materials

Purchased desk blotter
Patchwork blocks
Sheet of transparent plastic,
   cut ¼" smaller than blotter
FrayCheck™

Directions

1. Measure the purchased blotter. Remove the blotter paper.

2. Stitch the patchwork blocks together until they are the same size or larger than the blotter. Press all seams flat.

3. Trim the blocks ¼" smaller than the blotter dimensions. Stabilize all raw edges with FrayCheck; let dry.

4. Insert the patchwork corners into the blotter pockets. Insert the transparent plastic over the patchwork.

In the guest bedroom, antique quilts are enhanced by pillows and collectibles in soft pastel colors.

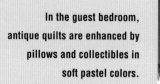

A small Yo-yo quilt hangs from a rack on the wall.

"Honey Bear" and "Courageous Lion," quilts from Christal's book *A Child's Garden of Quilts*, prowl in the hallway.

Miniature collectibles are grouped in shadow boxes for greater impact, then hung together on the dining room wall.

Below, left: Balls of various materials and sizes are displayed on wood bases and pedestals.

Below: Variations on a theme: a collection of eggs in front of a duck print

Mumm's the Word

Debbie Mumm—talented illustrator, designer, and author—lives with her husband, Steve, and son, Murphy, in a new home high on a hill, on the outskirts of Spokane, Washington.

Debbie's eye for color, along with her ability to create interesting arrangements of quilts, antiques, and hand-crafted objects, is evident in the vignettes throughout the house. She enjoys home decorating and incorporates the work of local artisans into many of the rooms.

Debbie readily accepted the challenge of creating a warm, inviting look from the builder's plain white walls and woodwork. She hired a local artist to soften those surfaces with faux finishes, and sponge and decorative painting. Debbie's designs also have been painted onto furniture and cabinet doors.

Located on the lower level of the home, Debbie's design studio is full of interesting antiques, quilts, and painted furniture, as well as fabric stashes and watercolors. Debbie works in watercolor to design her prints, posters, stationery, and fabric. These same designs can be found on kitchen and bath items, ceramic dinnerware and mugs, and various other gift and houseware lines. In this studio, she also creates the appealing quilts found in her books and Mumm's the Word patterns.

Opposite page: Debbie's studio, located on the lower level of the Mumm home, is chock full of interesting antiques, folk art, and a great collection of Mumm's the Word quilts. A large work table and bulletin board are located just off the seating area.

Left: An antique potting bench, complete with tin basin, holds painted flower pots and gardening tools along with Debbie's quilts and wall hangings. The trompe l'oeil painting on the wall replicates the look of brick behind peeling plaster.

Right: Debbie enjoys creating small vignettes within each room. In this corner, she combined an old screen door, garden trellis, and rake.

Above: Debbie's books and note cards are displayed on a tabletop in the work area of her studio. A quilt from her "Back to School" pattern decorates the table. Painted bricks emphasize the curved archway of the hearth.

Left: "Scrap Happy Flowers" and "Garden Baskets," two of Debbie's quilts, along with an assortment of books and painted objects, fill the tin-punched cupboard. Debbie's framed watercolor, "Santa's Teddy," sits next to a feather tree on top.

Above: The living room sofa and chairs feature a patchwork of upholstery fabrics: elegant brocade, brushed velvet, and striped ticking. The faux finish of the fireplace continues the woodwork and wainscoting treatment in the adjoining dining room.

Left: A corner cupboard holds an assortment of memorabilia, quilts, and topiary projects.

Above: *Mumm's the Word 10th Anniversary Book* contains an assortment of topiary projects that are easily incorporated into the garden theme of Debbie's dining room decor.

Left: A painted table, hand-crafted birdhouse, and floral-decorated twig chair fill the corner of the sunlit dining room. Faux finishes highlight the dining room wainscoting and woodwork.

Above: A tab valance, made with Debbie's fabric and fastened with antique buttons, was sewn by Retta Warehime. The button and yo-yo topiary trees are from *Mumm's the Word 10th Anniversary Book*.

Right: A hutch full of collectibles and small quilts forms a focal point in the breakfast room. The place mats, table runner, and napkins are "Yuletide Tables" designs from *Quick Country Christmas Quilts*.

Above: An overview of the comfortable family room focuses on the clever mantel and bookcase arrangements. The sampler quilt hanging above the fireplace is from *Mumm's the Word 10th Anniversary Book.*

Left: Two built-in oak shelves flank the fireplace and hold television and stereo equipment. To detract from the shiny new oak woodwork, Debbie removed several of the shelves and stacked old crates and boxes inside for displaying collectibles. Antique books, baskets, log houses, and colorful quilts help disguise the stereo and speakers.

Holiday Homecoming

Quilter Retta Warehime pulls out all the stops when she decorates her Kennewick, Washington, home for the holidays. Special decorations are placed in every room, including a theme tree in each of her children's bedrooms. Retta is active in her local quilt guild and other community-service groups, resulting in the inclusion of the Warehime home on various Christmas home tours. The house and garden have also been part of a garden tour and tea party.

Retta, a talented quilt designer and owner of Sew Cherished—a quilt pattern company—has many quilt samples in her bag of decorating tricks. Retta arranges these small quilted wall hangings in vignettes throughout the house and accents them with the folk-art pieces she collects and the antique furniture she inherited from her grandmother. A careful use of color and theme allows her to incorporate the wall hangings and collections into the overall decor of the room. Colors and themes are repeated in the decorative painting and stenciling she enjoys.

Retta writes her books and patterns from a small office near the ample family room. Her sewing room, shown on pages 186–87, is actually part of the family room, giving her more time with husband Dan and their children while she stitches up new creations. Retta's book *Seasoned with Quilts* (That Patchwork Place) attests to her creative stitching.

Opposite page:
Patchwork pillows and quilts bring a festive air to the living room Christmas decor. The collection of lighted houses in the curio cabinet and the Santa collection on top of the piano help to focus on the holiday at hand.

An original Santa crafted
by Leslie Beck greets guests
in the foyer.

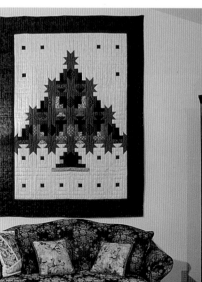

Above: Since the dining room is
one of the most prominent
rooms in the house and features
a territorial view, Retta
decorates a large tree for this
room and places it in the front
window. The floral fabrics in the
wall hanging match those used
for the valances.

Left: In the living room, a
Lighted Tree quilt by Retta
brightens the wall above the
love seat.

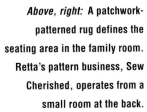

Above, right: A patchwork-patterned rug defines the seating area in the family room. Retta's pattern business, Sew Cherished, operates from a small room at the back.

Right: In an upstairs sitting room, a genuine Amish quilt purchased by Retta in Inter-course, Pennsylvania, inspired the window valance and shade.

Plaids and checks of various sizes and colors are combined to make cheery star quilts and pillow shams for the bunk beds in son Gregg's room. Retta stenciled stars on the dark blue ceiling and continued the star theme in the wallpaper border and small wall hanging (below).

Above and below: Retta chose a watermelon theme for daughter Marci's room and was able to use several wall hangings from her Sew Cherished pattern line. She painted the bench and stenciled a watermelon border near the ceiling.

Above and below: For daughter Jayme's room, Retta chose a sunflower motif and echoed the design on the patchwork pillow and wall hanging. Smaller wooden sunflowers are found throughout the room, and dried sunflowers decorate the small Christmas tree. Retta made the picket-fence headboard and the Star and Chain quilt on the bed.

Decorator Touches

Holiday Pomanders

Materials

8 oranges, unpeeled
3 cups whole cloves
2 cups orrisroot powder*
1 cup ground cinnamon
¾ cup ground allspice
½ cup ground nutmeg
Small cardboard box
Tissue paper

Available at your local pharmacy

Directions

1. Lightly draw a design on the orange with a pencil.
2. Insert the cloves by hand. It will be easier to insert cloves if you use a large darning needle to poke holes in the orange rind first. Allow ⅛" between cloves, since the orange will shrink as it dries.
3. Blend the orrisroot and spices, then roll the clove-studded oranges in the spice mixture.
4. Put the oranges in the cardboard box lined with tissue paper. Pour the remaining spice mixture over the oranges, covering the bottom of the box. Cover the box and store it in a warm (not hot), dry place for 3 to 4 weeks. Avoid humidity and extreme warmth.
5. When the oranges are thoroughly dry, shake off the excess powder. Your holiday pomanders are now ready to use in a decorative arrangement.

Oranges studded with cloves have an unusual, festive look and fill your kitchen with a subtle fragrance.

Right: Longaberger baskets hanging from the ceiling rack, and pine shelves full of patchwork-patterned dishes add charm to the kitchen and eating area. A Star of Wonder table runner and quilt are used for extra spots of holiday color.

Decorator Touches

Shower Curtain (72" x 72")

In this bathroom decorated with a birdhouse theme, an appliqué design is enlarged and stitched onto the shower curtain.

Materials

4½ yds. fabric for background (add an extra ½ yd. to match plaids or stripes)
Appliqué pattern of your choice
Scraps of fabric for appliqué
Fusible bonding material (HeatnBond®, Wonder-Under®)
Purchased shower-curtain liner

Directions

1. Cut the background fabric into two 80" lengths. The extra 8" allows a double 1" top hem and a double 3" bottom hem. When cutting the second piece, adjust placement of the cut so the pattern, if any, will match along the selvages.

2. Pin the pieces along one long edge, with right sides together and pattern matching. Stitch a ½"-wide seam, then press the seam open.

3. Turn the side edges under ¼". Press. Turn under again ¼". Stitch close to the pressed edge.

4. Turn the top edge under 1". Press. Turn under again 1". Stitch close to the pressed edge.

5. Turn the bottom edge under 3". Press. Turn under again 3". Stitch close to pressed edge.

6. Following the directions given with the appliqué pattern and using bonding material, prepare scraps of fabric for appliqué. Fuse in place, then stitch around the edges to secure.

7. To mark the buttonhole placement, align the purchased liner with the fabric curtain and mark a vertical line at each hole in the liner. Stitch buttonholes, following the directions for your sewing machine.

Birdhouses are the theme in the downstairs powder room. A birdhouse wall hanging decorates one wall, repeating the theme of the Christmas tree and tree skirt. Additional hand-crafted birdhouses in a variety of sizes and styles fill out the room.

Painted to Perfection

*T*he traditional façade of Kathy and Dave Renzelman's home, located in a Virginia suburb of Washington, D.C., gives little hint of the delightful surprises waiting inside. Kathy, a decorative painter, has added light, whimsical touches throughout the house. She uses trompe l'oeil to decorate doors, tabletops, cupboards, and walls. Interspersed with these touches are wall hangings, quilts, and other collected treasures.

Kathy enjoys making small theme quilts and includes them as part of the decorating vignettes she arranges in each room. She has an eye for grouping just the right accents and collectibles together. Her collections include birdhouses, baskets, and Noah's arks (see page 178).

Dave, a research scientist, is retired from the military. Frequent relocations gave Kathy an opportunity to collect a variety of interesting objects and to fine-tune her decorating skills as she adapted existing furniture to new locations.

Opposite page:
Baskets, birdhouses, wall hangings, and quilts are displayed in abundance in the family room; Kathy ties them all together with her favorite color—blue.

Below: Birdhouses perch on top of an entertainment cabinet, while the shelves and drawers hold decorative items and wall hangings. It's hard to spot the television amidst these intriguing items.

Above: A homey fireplace screen warms the hearth. Echoing the house theme, a stack of pantry boxes, painted by Kathy, is topped with a collectible wooden house. Handmade quilts and pillows complete the scene.

Right: In front of a simple blue-and-white–striped sofa, the coffee table is filled with decorative items and quilts.

Right: Painted cupboard doors portray a neat and tidy pantry.

Above: Ruffled borders are painted on the tabletop, chair seats, and chair backs for a feminine touch.

Above: An antique cart filled with quilts rests beside a wing chair softened with quilts and pillows.

The master bathroom features a high ledge on which plants and collectibles can be displayed. Kathy lets antiques and dried flower arrangements color this mostly white bathroom, which is brightened by brass fixtures and accents.

Decorator Touches

A Painted Garden

A painted garden hides inside the master bathroom.

Materials

White flat latex wall paint
Beige accent paint
Large sponge
Small containers of decorative paint
  for flowers
Old wooden window frame
Silk flowers

Directions

1. Paint the walls with the white paint. Allow to dry.
2. Using the sponge and beige accent paint, evenly sponge the paint onto the walls.
3. Paint flowers and plants around the baseboard, using the decorative paint.
4. Hang the old window frame on the wall. Add silk flowers for a window-box effect.
5. *Optional:* Accent with baskets of flowers.

Painted birdhouses decorate the door panels of this powder room, setting the stage for the avian theme inside.

Above: Appliquéd guest towels complement wall hangings featuring birds and birdhouses.

Left: A decorative painting entitled "Company Picnic" and a celestial-theme chair turn a plain hallway into a destination.

New England Odyssey

*T*he Village House, a country bed-and-breakfast inn in Sutton Mills, New Hampshire, provides the perfect setting for quilt display. Owned and renovated by Peggy and Norm Forand, the inn has plenty of rooms, as well as nooks and crannies, in which to display quilts.

When Norm retired from running his own manufacturing firm and Peggy from her nursing career, the couple left the Philadelphia area and headed north to New England in search of a bed-and-breakfast for sale. As luck would have it, they came upon the ideal place and quickly settled in to renovate. Now adorned with Peggy's quilts and Norm's handiwork, the home provides a welcome setting for visitors year 'round.

An avid quilter, Peggy often hosts meetings of her quilt group, Windham Quilters Anonymous, around the dining room table. The quilts stitched by this group and other quilts by That Patchwork Place author Carol Doak brighten the inn's decor.

Opposite page: Quilts abound in this light-filled dining room, including appliquéd pie place mats by Windham Quilters Anonymous (inset). A scrap quilt hangs on a quilt rack, and a corner cupboard is filled with quilts.

Above: "Father Christmas," made by Peggy, presides over the plaid-skirted table.

Above: In an upstairs hallway, a sampler quilt by Carol Doak and a Sailboat quilt by Peggy cozy up a child's cradle. A patchwork bib and a collection of Raggedy Ann and Andy dolls complete the scene.

Left: Red-and-green quilts color
the hallway at Christmastime.

Red-and-white quilts and pillows continue the
Christmas theme at the top of the stairs. A Feathered
Star Medallion quilt by Ginny Guaraldi hangs next to
a Schoolhouse quilt by Peggy.

Antique Postage Stamp quilts on the twin beds are complemented by antique quilts from the collections of Terry Maddox and the Forands. The "Peace and Love" quilt on the wall was made by Mary Kay Sieve.

Hearts of all sizes and shapes enliven this perky powder room. Delicate paper-pieced quilts by Pam Ludwig and Carol Doak warm the walls and the painted wooden chair.

Left: More antique quilts from the Forands' collection make this small single bedroom inviting. Pam Ludwig made the miniature Fan quilt on the wall.

Below: Colorful scrap quilts brighten this cozy room with rich green walls and warm pine floors.

A Colorful Contemporary

*T*he contemporary home of Ann and Mel Stohl in Yakima, Washington, abounds with colorful quilts and souvenirs of their travels. Mel, a retired physician, and Ann, a former quilt-shop owner, spend a great deal of time traveling. Ann's expert eye is always on the alert for antiques and unusual items. Once Ann arrives home with these new finds, her sense of style and eye for arrangement create exciting vignettes.

Ann enjoys gardening, flower arranging, and needlepoint, so it's not surprising that floral themes abound throughout the house. She enjoys collecting costumes as well as quilts, and the large-scale rooms of her home provide the perfect setting for their display.

The home's interior is filled with an eclectic mix of antiques, heirloom furniture, and a variety of textiles. Ann's collection of antique quilts is vast, and she readily shares her treasures with others. Many of these quilts have been photographed for use in That Patchwork Place books, displayed in museums, or loaned for exhibits.

Opposite page: The main living area, filled with quilts and collectibles, encompasses several sitting areas and a dining area.

Right: An antique Tulip quilt hangs in the stairwell behind an arrangement of fresh tulips.

Below: On the dining table, an Anvil quilt is topped with a protective piece of glass, then an arrangement of sparkling candlesticks, crystal, and a blooming orchid. A Four Patch scrap quilt hangs over the door of the armoire.

Needlepoint pillows stitched by Ann reflect the colors
of the bright Lone Star quilt on the wall.

Below: Quilts are stacked
in an open cupboard near a
quilt-covered chair.

Above: The quilt-covered chair looks
inviting beside a trunk filled with
pillows and textile treasures.

Above: An antique Oak Leaf
appliqué quilt is folded at the
foot of the bed. More needlepoint pillows coordinate with
the striped shams and Ralph
Lauren florals.

A bed canopy of sheer lace
strikes a romantic note.

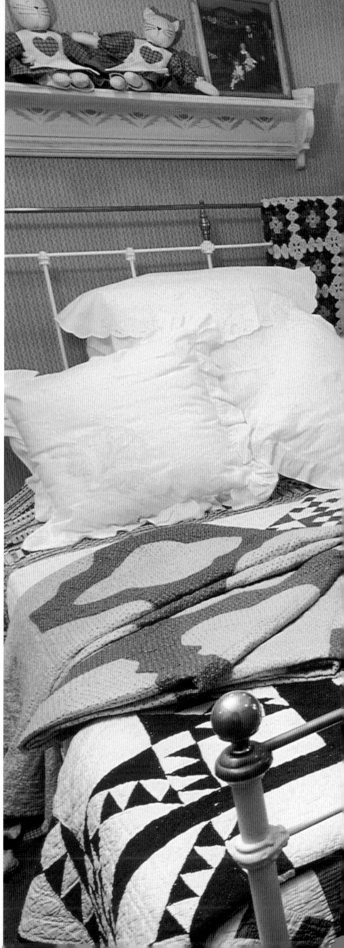

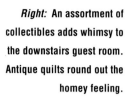

Right: An assortment of collectibles adds whimsy to the downstairs guest room. Antique quilts round out the homey feeling.

Dolls and teddy bears in chairs sit on one of the twin beds, ready to greet visitors.

Right: Twig furniture contrasts with fine lace, crystal, floral prints, and colorful quilts on this deck set for an outdoor tea party.

Left: Ann's quilt collection mixes nicely on shelves with pottery and dishes.

114

As quiltmaking has grown in popularity, so has quilt collecting. A renewed interest in Americana and handmade objects has also focused attention on quilts. Major museum exhibitions as well as national quilt shows have brought rare and sought-after quilts to the attention of the collecting public.

A new breed of collector whose sole interest is quilt collecting has emerged. Major private collections are being shared with the quilting world. These collections, whether large or small, record the history of quilting from past to present. The owners of these collections are committed to not only the preservation of quilts, but also their history. Documentation and research not only enhance the value of these collections, but foster appreciation of our quilt heritage.

In this section of the book, you'll find a variety of quilt collections gathered by enthusiasts with a common vision of preserving quilt history. Their collecting philosophies vary, but they are all open to sharing their treasures with fellow quilters, scholars, and historians.

A Victory quilt made to celebrate the end of World War II hangs in the stairwell of Alice Berg's home.

A Diverse Collection

Sharon Evans Yenter, owner of In The Beginning, a truly amazing quilt and fabric shop in Seattle, Washington, has used a wide variety of quilts to decorate her top-floor condominium. The quilts range from exhilarating contemporary quilts by artists such as Erika Carter and Jason Yenter, to heavily quilted traditional antique patterns and romantic pastel quilts crafted from Sharon's new line of fabrics. Each quilt is carefully integrated into the room's decor, holding its own against the magnificent 180° views of the Seattle skyline.

Sharon has collected quilts for more than twenty years. She often displays her quilts in the shop or allows them to be displayed as part of a fundraising activity. Several of her antique quilts served as inspiration for new quilt designs featured in her book, *In The Beginning*.

Sharon collects all types of quilts, even "ratty" ones. She feels someone spent a lot of time thinking, talking, and daydreaming over each quilt, so each and every one is special. Sharon especially enjoys what she refers to as the "break-out" quilts: wild and wondrous creations made by adventuresome women who lived in a rigid society. Most of these quilts are in mint condition, perhaps because they lay unused in drawers for years after someone exclaimed, "Oh, look what Aunt Maude gave us, dear." The eccentricities of the Aunt Maudes of the world live on in these quilts, and Sharon appreciates their charm and the "I-can-do-it" attitude they invoke.

Sharon shares her interest in quilts with her husband, Bill, and son Jason, who manages In The Beginning and is a renowned quiltmaker in his own right.

Right: A miniature kimono in Japanese fabrics by Jason Yenter is framed in a shadowbox and enhanced by a collection of Japanese porcelain. Porcelain cats dressed in traditional Japanese garb complete the vignette.

The graphic, contemporary "Firedance" hangs above the sofa in the living room and serves as a focal point in a room full of traditional furniture and floor-to-ceiling views. Made by Jason Yenter in 1992, the wall hanging is pieced from hand-dyed fabric.

In the master bedroom, an antique Carolina Lily quilt serves as a headboard, while an antique Grandmother's Dream quilt is folded at the foot of the bed.

Below: Detail of Grandmother's Dream quilt

Above: Perched on the pencil-post bed, one feels high above the clouds in this cozy guest room. The bed is spread with a Trip Around the World quilt by Sue Pilarski. Sue used Sharon's In The Beginning line of fabrics, produced by Northcott Fabrics. Next to the bed, antique quilts hang on a rack.

Left: Sue Pilarski also made the Trip Around the World quilt on the wall, a perfect choice for this lofty retreat.

Midwest Treasure Trove

Mary and Roger Ghromley live in a comfortable, turn-of-the-century home on a tree-lined street in Lincoln, Nebraska. Mary, an accomplished quilter, loves to reproduce the patterns found in old quilts. Her collection numbers more than one hundred quilts (more than two hundred if you also count her miniature and doll quilts). Her interest in quilting has been lifelong, and her contributions to the Nebraska Quilt Project and the Nebraska Quilt Preservation Project have been invaluable.

Mary has been an avid quilt collector since the mid-1970s. Her collection focuses on two distinct types of quilts: antique and miniature. To go with the miniature quilts, she also collects miniature doll beds and antique children's dresses. The textiles in some of the dresses help her assign dates to quilts in her collection.

You'll often find Roger driving Mary in search of another quilt for her collection or delivering her to various speaking engagements, carrying the bags of quilts she uses to illustrate her talks. But this retired telephone executive has his own collection of antique telephones and posters.

Opposite page: An antique red-and-green quilt graces the dining room table during the Christmas holidays.

Right: In the living room, an antique Chips and Whetstones quilt hangs above the sofa. Mary was attracted by the appliqué border and the Prussian blue fabric in the blocks. A Wild Goose Chase quilt is folded over the sofa back, and an antique Pyramids quilt drapes over the chair.

Right: The upstairs bedrooms, once occupied by the Ghromleys' four daughters, now hold a variety of beds and quilts to welcome returning children and grandchildren. Matching pink-and-white Drunkard's Path quilts cover the twin beds. A Basket quilt is folded at the foot of one bed, and antique doll quilts fill the wall space.

Above: Antique crib quilts are grouped around an old iron crib. Peeking out from underneath the crib are three vintage doll beds, each spread with an antique doll quilt.

Right: A Chain quilt hangs on the wall above the iron bedstead, and an appliqué quilt is folded at the foot of the bed. Miniature Log Cabin quilts march down the stairway to the main floor.

Children's dresses from yesteryear hang from the headboard of this youth bed. More miniature quilts are folded in the trunk and in the cradle.

An upstairs bedroom and its adjoining alcove hold a treasure trove of doll beds and miniature quilts. These hard-to-find beds are excellent for displaying miniature quilts.

An antique Nine Patch quilt dresses a table on the back porch. Collections,
including Raggedy Ann and Andy dolls, brighten up the space.

Mary also collects blue glass,
which sparkles as the sun enters
the dining room window.

Above: Detail of hand-pieced
pillowcases

A real treasure is found on
this antique bed: a pieced
Basket quilt and coordinating,
hand-stitched pillowcases.
The decorative edge on the
pillowcases took time—a sure
sign that these linens were
saved for special occasions
and seldom used.

The James Collection

$\mathcal{I}$magine living in a home filled with more than one thousand quilts of every persuasion, from rare antiques to modern art. Ardis and Robert James live in such a home in Westchester County, New York. Their rambling Colonial houses one of the world's largest and most distinguished private quilt collections.

When the collection grew beyond the bounds of the house, the Jameses added a custom-designed gallery. Connected to the main house by a glassed-in porch, the gallery holds quilts on specially designed storage platforms. Light, humidity, and temperature are all electronically controlled. Here one finds rare Baltimore Album quilts, Amish quilts, and vintage quilts alongside the work of contemporary artists such as Michael James, Terrie Hancock Mangat, Nancy Crow, and Pamela Studstill.

The Jameses take custodianship seriously, employing a photographer to document their collection at regular intervals. A curator regularly updates the notebooks that contain photos and documentary information about each quilt.

In addition to *collecting* quilts, Ardis creates her own—mostly traditional quilts and quilted clothing. Indeed, her basement workroom is a treasure trove of old lace, odd bits of fabric, and vintage textiles.

Robert, a former college professor and successful businessman, shares Ardis's love of quilts and plays an active part in acquiring new quilts for their collection.

Right: An overview of the gallery reveals four specially designed platforms storing a magnificent collection of quilts. Hanging on the walls (left to right) are works by Terrie Hancock Mangat, and Michael James, an antique quilt with a celestial theme, a friendship appliqué quilt, a hand-dyed piece by Jan Myers-Newbury, and an antique Crazy quilt.

Two sofas are placed back to back in the center of the room for visitors. On the coffee table are documentation albums for the Jameses' collection.

Above: "The Calendar Fetish—
An Alter to Time" is an actual
working calendar by Susan Shie.

Right: More storage platforms
slide out from under the bed.

Above: An antique friendship appliqué quilt hangs next to "Depth of Field III: Plane View" by Jan Myers-Newbury.

Left: Notebooks of photos and documentary information

Ardis created the strip-pieced table cover used in the breakfast nook. On the wall, she placed "A View into Time/Motion" by Michael James. Michael James's work was their first contemporary acquisition, and the Jameses now own six of his pieces.

Above: A collection of bottles helps mask the air conditioner. Robert's mother, Cora James, made the weaving that serves as a backdrop for the bottle collection.

In the living room, a chair fittingly upholstered in a patchwork of fabrics is placed near the fireplace. "Memory Jars" by Terrie Hancock Mangat hangs on the wall.

Left: Ardis used a different-color carpet on each stair for a patchwork effect. The bright colors balance the antique wool Robbing Peter to Pay Paul quilt, which hangs below the work of Pamela Studstill. On the adjacent wall is "Mexican Graveyard" by Terrie Hancock Mangat.

Below: In the front hallway, a small piece by Laura Munson Reinstatler, "Reciprocation," hangs on the wall.

131

A Bright and Sunny Outlook

*T*racey and Mick McHugh's Mercer Island, Washington, home is full of antique quilts she has collected, bright little wall hangings she has stitched, and colorful quilts crafted by their children and their classmates. The house is alive with a joyous sense of color.

Tracey feels there are many reasons to collect quilts. She appreciates their tactile comforts, graphic designs, vintage fabrics, and the personal stories or signatures they carry. Tracey especially likes to collect homey, quirky quilts, like those made in the l930s. She looks for quilts with quality workmanship and in good condition, but often finds herself purchasing an old, worn quilt just to rescue it. These quilts are displayed on a rotating basis throughout the home, along with newer, more colorful pieces.

Mick, owner of several fine restaurants in the Seattle area, shares Tracey's enthusiasm for quilts, as do their four children. Tracey has been a frequent visitor to the kids' classrooms, where she has taught quiltmaking and engineered several school fund-raising projects. She stitches the children's blocks into quilts, then auctions the quilts to raise money for the school. Tracey becomes so involved in these projects and so enamored of the quilts that she is often the highest bidder.

Opposite page: Antique quilts and brightly colored pillows fill the window seat in the eating area.

Left: A folksy doll rests on top of a folded antique Double Wedding Ring quilt. China and pottery stored in the hutch coordinate with the House wall hanging made by Tracey.

The Log Cabin quilt folded over
the sofa back and the Four Patch
quilt on the love seat enliven this
contemporary living room.

Above: Several antique quilts give a cozy look to this corner of the bedroom. A Basket quilt covers the chair and coordinates with the patchwork and appliqué quilts layered over the table.

Right: In the master bedroom, a collection of 1930s quilts and vintage linens coordinate with the gaily striped bed skirt and comforter lining. Butterfly quilts add a bold, graphic touch.

Above: An appliquéd Coffee Cup quilt invites friends to a coffee klatch in the kitchen.

Right: In the back entryway of the house, a quilt made in daughter Emma's class at Seattle Country Day School hangs on the wall behind a wagonload of bears and a Sailboat quilt made by Tracey.

Part 3
All Through the House

*Of time within the home well spent,
the heart with homely tasks contents.*
—PATCHWORK COVERLET

Quilts and collections are an excellent way to introduce yourself and your home to visitors. The objects you collect and choose to display in your home reveal much about you and your family. Instead of relegating these collectibles to private rooms and spaces, let them appear throughout the house. They can serve as a focal point in a room and help create a sense of warmth and comfort, surrounding visitors with things you admire and enjoy.

Each room in a house traditionally fills a specific need: a place to sleep, a place to eat, or a place to entertain. Don't let traditional room functions deter you as you plan the use of your interior space. In separate columns on a piece of paper, list your space needs and the names of the available rooms in your home. If you have more needs than rooms, try making several of your rooms multipurpose areas. For instance, a formal dining room can also house a library, serve as a den or study, or become a sewing studio. Since the eating area in my keeping room is quite large and most of my entertaining involves buffet-style meals, I eliminated my formal dining room years ago. Instead, I use this area as a cozy library and den. Keep an open mind about room function as you view the rooms on the following pages. It may be possible to create new spaces that serve several needs.

In Susan and Roger Morin's guest house, the arched wooden door and apothecary chest are bathed in mellow light. A hooked entry rug spells out the message, "Welcome Friends."

> *To the house of a friend
> is never far.*
> —UNKNOWN

A Grand Entrance

*E*ntryways inside and out welcome guests and create a first impression. These same entryways also welcome the family home each evening or after a long trip, surrounding us with familiar and beloved quilts and objects.

Viewing the foyer of Susan and Roger Morin's home from above emphasizes the warm tones of the gleaming tile floor, parquetry landing, and luminous hardwood stairs. Folk-art collectibles surround a hooked rug made by Susan.

Left: Pots of geraniums and a hooked rug brighten the entryway of Alice and Wally Berg's home. The door opens onto a small foyer, where a Churn Dash quilt made by Alice hangs above a primitive bench and doll.

Above: Miniature quilts and Santas are tucked into baskets, and a collection of old books is stacked on the floor.

Right: The foyer of Terry Guizzo's Kennewick, Washington, home invokes a warm, nostalgic mood as she welcomes the holiday season. An old typewriter holds the newsletter from her quilt shop, Pieceable Dry Goods, while lace doilies and antique linens spill from the drawers.

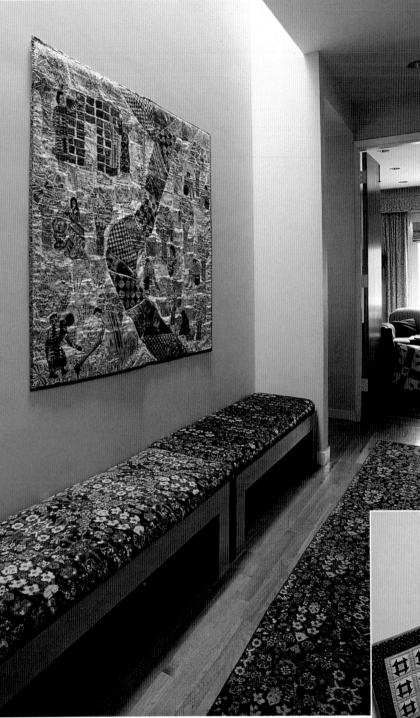

Hallways are a home decorator's biggest challenge; their long, narrow dimensions leave little room for furniture. Stairways pose the same problem, with the additional challenge of added ceiling height. With their versatility, compactness, and freedom from function, quilts and collections rise to the occasion, delightfully dressing these awkward spaces.

Below: To spotlight her interest in gardening, Cleo Nollette built a picket fence to decorate the stairway ledge in her Seattle home. Miniature quilts by Mary Hickey hang above dolls, birdhouses, gardening books, and seed packets.

Above: This hallway in the home of Lee and Robert Porter has an alcove that accommodates an upholstered bench customized to coordinate with the rug. "By the Waters of Babylon," a pictorial quilt based on Jeremiah and Psalm 137, hangs on the wall.

140

The first-floor hallway of the Porter home features an antique Le Moyne Star quilt mounted on a muslin base. (See directions at right.)

Decorator Touches
Stabilizing and Displaying an Antique Quilt

Detail of Le Moyne Star quilt

Many antique quilts cannot withstand the stress of hanging without a support system to stabilize them. In addition, a stabilized backing evens out the wavy edges of antique quilts that have been heavily quilted. Lee Porter used the following method to stabilize her antique Le Moyne Star quilt.

Materials

4 pieces of 1" x 1" lumber (length depends on quilt dimensions)
Muslin (amount depends on quilt dimensions)
Staple gun and staples
Needle and thread

Directions

1. Build a wood frame from 1" x 1" lumber, approximately 4" larger than the quilt (80" x 80" for a 76" x 76" quilt).
2. Cut and seam the muslin to make a large piece approximately 5" larger than the wood frame (85" x 85" in the example).
3. Get someone to help you stretch the muslin tightly around the frame. Staple the muslin to the back side of the frame on all 4 sides. Trim any excess fabric.
4. Place the quilt on top of the muslin backing, leaving an equal amount of muslin showing on all sides and smoothing the edges.
5. Using a needle and 2 strands of thread, hand stitch the quilt edges to the muslin.

*No matter where
I serve my guests,
they seem to like
my kitchen best.*

—UNKNOWN

The Heart of the Home

$\mathcal{I}$t's true that the kitchen is the usual gathering place for both family and guests. Warmth and good smells emanate from it as food is being prepared, attracting the hungry and the curious. Here the day's events can be shared as children return from school, and parents from work or daily activities. It's important, then, to decorate this oft-used room invitingly. Since wall space is limited, use small wall hangings or place mats for bright spots of color. This is also a good place to display collections, whether kitchen related or not.

The all-white kitchen of Karen and Charlie Snyder benefits from color in the form of miniature quilts, blue linens and crockery, and a big pot of red geraniums.

A chicken-and-egg theme feathers the kitchen of
Alice and Wally Berg. Bright red accents against
a background of hunter green–checked wallpaper
enliven the plain cabinets and appliances.

A corner bookcase in the same
kitchen holds cookbooks,
collectibles, and a miniature
quilt made by Alice.

The newly remodeled kitchen in Joan and Jim Hanson's Seattle home is a cook's dream. The warm wood of the cabinets and floor contrast with the cool tones of the countertops and tiles. Joan's collection of Fiesta dishes virtually glows in this setting. She saved the cutoff selvages of her quilting fabrics and crocheted the strips into colorful place mats for the table.

In the back hallway hang two sentimental quilts Joan made from blocks her mother embroidered as a young girl. Birdhouses, miniature tea sets, and one of Joan's childhood dolls complete the scene.

Left: A lively purple color scheme sets off beautiful mahogany cabinets in the Shepherd House Inn bed-and-breakfast in Kennewick, Washington. High ceilings accommodate large glass-fronted cupboards, leaving plenty of room for collectibles on top. Owner Karen Cadwell papered the ceiling with a tiny floral wallpaper print, hand cutting the motif to trail down the walls above the cabinet. The corner area is left open for a basket of tulips with an uplight added for drama. The purple Grape Basket quilt draped over the center island adds a colorful accent for special occasions.

Above: Rosemary and Harold Youmans's Atlanta, Georgia, dining room boasts Williamsburg Colonial furniture and accessories. "Remember Me," an American crib quilt from Little Quilts, covers the table.

*A house becomes a home
when each room is filled with love.*

—UNKNOWN

Living It Up

*L*iving rooms are gathering places for family and friends. In the case of homes without family rooms, the living room is usually decorated in a more casual style, allowing for family relaxation as well as formal entertaining. The rooms shown on these pages serve both functions and also make room for quilts and collections.

Earthy textures, a mix of casual fabrics, and wicker furniture invite guests to sit and stay awhile. Slipcovers and tab curtains with a relaxed fit ease the formality of a room, as does a loosely arranged bouquet of flowers in an unusual container.

Left: A bright scrap quilt drapes gracefully over the sofa back in the living room of Joan and Jim Hanson. An antique bird cage filled with quilts is placed in the foyer, visible through the curved archways. Next to the bird cage is "Garland Star" by Judy Pollard.

Below: A glass-top coffee table displays collectibles, including children's books and crocheted potholders that look like dresses.

Left: In the living room of Dan and Nancy Martin's beach cottage, slipcovers brighten the living room during the summer months. Nancy selected the coordinating prints, then had Mary Terry of Esther's Fabrics on Bainbridge Island, Washington, stitch them. The red and green checks used for the sofa and love seat backs coordinate with the plaid cushions and geranium-print pillows. The geranium print appears again on the seat of the easy chair and the ruffled skirts of the ottomans. A Double Wedding Ring quilt from the 1930s, red-and-green Honeymoon Cottage and Bed of Peonies quilts, and vintage textiles are cheerful accents. Casual arrangements of flowers fill old canning jars grouped in a wire carrier.

Left: Warm red walls in Terry Guizzo's living room form a glowing backdrop for holiday decorations. The large-scale plaid used on the sofa coordinates with a smaller plaid on the wing chair. Patchwork pillows cluster on the sofa, and a bouquet of quilts is gathered with a raffia bow and hung informally on the wall at left. An Amish quilt covers the dining room table in the foreground, and an antique quilt does duty as a tree skirt.

Santas are arranged on a glass-top table next to a wing chair adorned with appliqué pillows and a small quilt. Note how the plaid theme is repeated in the curtain panels. Collectibles fill a corner cupboard.

*The bed, my friend, is our whole life.
It is there that we are born, it is there
that we love, it is there that we die.*

—GUY DE MAUPASSANT

Snuggle Up

The bedroom is more than a place for sleeping. It has become a private retreat where one can retire to read, relax, watch television, or pursue hobbies. Once a small, sparsely decorated room, today's bedroom has a well-coordinated, opulent look. Creature comforts abound—plump pillows, soft comforters, and cozy quilts—providing solace and a respite from a harried, high-tech world.

Left: A small star wall hanging echoes the cutouts on the headboard.

Below: More stars appear on the lampshade and the walls. Terry sponge-painted the walls (below and opposite), then highlighted them with decorative stenciling. After painting the chest, headboard, and folding screen she designed and commissioned, she applied a hand-rubbed finish.

Left: A star-spangled theme prevails in the master suite of Terry Guizzo's home. Continuing the folk-art look of the rest of the house (see pages 148–49), stars appear on a sampler quilt, as decorative cutouts on a folding screen, and as stencils above a doorway. Birdhouses and other interesting accessories are tucked into nooks and crannies.

LET ME LIVE IN THE HOUSE
BY THE SIDE OF THE ROAD
AND BE A FRIEND TO MAN

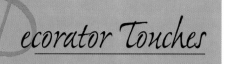

Decorator Touches

Triangular Valance

Joan Hanson made this pretty valance from two coordinating fabrics, outlining each section with contrasting trim. The size and shape of the triangular pieces were determined by the ribbon-swirl pattern in the floral print. Joan hung the finished sections from a muslin-covered board.

A decorative valance conceals raised Levolor blinds, opens the room to the view, and draws attention to the custom windows.

Materials

Floral print fabric
Yellow striped fabric
Contrasting blue solid fabric for trim
1" x 2" cedar board, 2" longer than width
   of window frame
Waterproof opaque
   drapery-lining fabric
2 L brackets for mounting the valance
Staple gun and staples
Paper for pattern

Directions

1. Measure the window frame and add 2" to that measurement.

2. Select a motif or section of the floral fabric to repeat on the triangular valance piece. Make a paper pattern of this shape and measure the width.

3. Determine how many triangular sections you want to use and where they will fall on the window design. In this case, the motifs are spaced to fall in the center of each window and to overlap the yellow sections. At each end of the valance, a half triangle is used.

4. Using the paper pattern as a guide, cut valance sections from both the floral and contrasting fabrics. Cut linings for each piece from the lining material.

5. From the yellow striped fabric, cut bias strips 1½" wide and long enough to trim the outside edge of a triangle. Cut 1 yellow bias strip for every floral triangle. Fold each strip in half lengthwise, wrong sides together, and press flat.

6. On the right side of each floral triangle, baste a yellow bias strip to the outside edge, keeping raw edges even and gently curving the lower corner. Clip the fabric to accommodate the curve.

7. Match the lining fabric to the floral fabric, right sides together, and pin. Stitch the lining to the floral fabric, using the basting line as a stitching guide. Clip the curves. Turn right side out and press.

8. Repeat steps 5–7 using yellow triangles and blue solid bias strips.

9. Cover the cedar board with drapery-lining fabric.

10. Staple triangles to the 2" side of the fabric-covered board, alternating striped and floral pieces and using a half triangle at each end. Overlap each piece by the same amount.

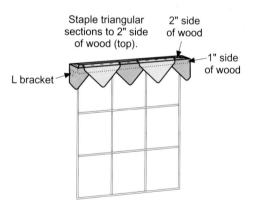

Staple triangular sections to 2" side of wood (top).

2" side of wood

1" side of wood

L bracket

11. Hang with L brackets at each end of the valance. Note that the 1" edge of the board will rest against the wall. This allows the valance to project out over the window trim and to cover blinds or other hardware.

Joan and Jim Hanson's master bedroom features a cheery yellow color scheme. Indeed, the name of the quilt on the bed is "Cheerful Child." Joan made the fabric-covered headboard, the wall hanging, and the decorative pillow shams to coordinate with the blue carpet and her mother's blue-and-white china. White accents liven up the room even more.

This warm and cozy bedroom in the beach cottage of Nancy and Dan Martin prominently features two quilts: Amsterdam Star on the wall and Pinwheel Squares on the bed. When winter weather calls for a duvet on the bed, Nancy casually drapes a smaller quilt over the corner. The large-scale print of the duvet cover provides a perfect backdrop for a bed full of pillows. The mirrored closet doors reflect the myriad patterns.

Patchwork pillows take a seat on a cushion with tied ends, softening the primitive twig chair.

Decorator Touches

Pretty Pillowcases

One of the easiest ways to add color to a bedroom is with pillowcases in a variety of decorative fabrics. Change the pillowcases frequently to coordinate with the small pillows and to add seasonal or holiday touches.

Materials for 2 pillowcases

1½ yds. main fabric
¾ yd. fabric for trim
2½ yds. contrasting piping

Directions

1. Cut a piece of the main fabric 24" x 42".
2. Cut a piece of the trim fabric 13" x 42".
3. Baste piping to one long edge of the main fabric.
4. Stitch the trim fabric to the main fabric, using the basting line as a stitching guide. Press toward the trim.
5. Turn the raw edge under ¼" along the remaining long edge of the trim. Press.
6. Fold the trim to the inside, covering the stitching. Press.
7. On the outside of the case, topstitch in-the-ditch along the piping, catching the turned-under edge of the trim.
8. To finish the pillowcase with a French seam:
   a. Fold the stitched fabric in half crosswise, *wrong sides together.*
   b. Stitch along the top and side edges, using a ¼"-wide seam allowance.
   c. Turn the pillowcase inside out, right sides together.
   d. Stitch, using a ½"-wide seam allowance.
   e. Turn the pillowcase right side out and press.
9. Repeat steps 1–8 to make the second pillowcase.

Right: A perky yellow-and-white striped wallpaper, accented with a Laura Ashley shade and wallpaper border, complements the soft buttery yellows of the 1930s quilts—a perfect bed-and-breakfast setting in Shepherd House Inn.

Below: A vintage Bow Tie quilt top is folded at the foot of the bed in the Williamsburg-style bedroom of Rosemary and Harold Youmans. Wooden blinds admit a soft glow of light.

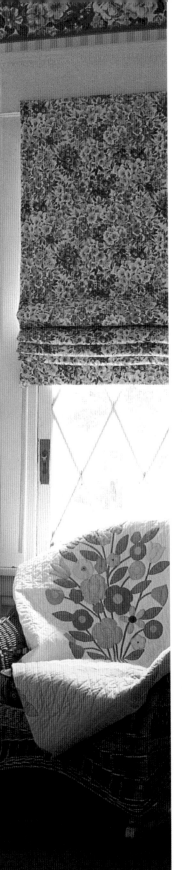

Right: Cleo Nollette's light-filled bedroom mixes perky stripes and checks with a large-scale floral print. Cleo re-covered the kitchen chair, transforming an ugly duckling into a graceful swan worthy of this feminine retreat.

A custom window treatment frames a view of the water, and miniblinds control light and privacy.

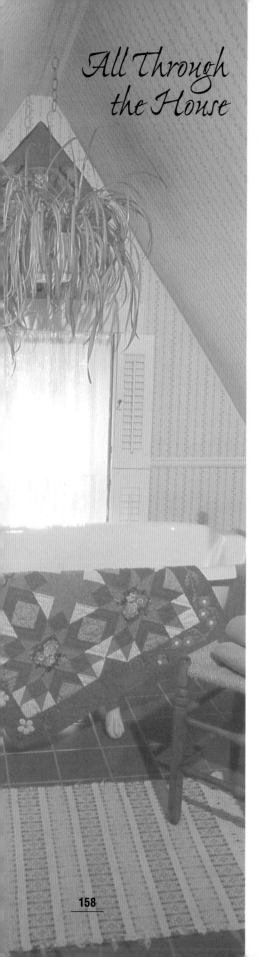

A hundred men may make an encampment, but it takes a woman to make a home.

—CHINESE PROVERB

The Decorated Bath

Decorating bathrooms for pleasure is another phenomenon of the '90s. Bathrooms are now expected to be both functional and decorative, relaxing spots where we can rejuvenate body and spirit. Thus, it's not surprising to see small wall hangings and decorative painting show up in this oft-visited room.

An old-fashioned claw-foot tub fills the dormer of the upstairs bath in Peggy and Norm Forand's New England bed-and-breakfast. Plush towels, a small quilt, and a hanging plant add a cozy feeling.

The marbled walls and rich wood wainscoting in a guest bathroom at the Sheppard House Inn enrich the vintage tile floor. A trompe l'oeil bookcase on the far wall echoes the colors of the quilt and needlepoint stool.

A floral fabric sets the theme in Terry Guizzo's painted bathroom. Corrugated cardboard was used to stamp a background design on the wall, which was then embellished with hand-painted flowers to match the curtains. Bright towels tied with strips of fabric add a splash of color, as do the picket-fence shelf and other garden accents.

The powder room in Pieceable Dry Goods quilt shop features a stamped border with a star motif to complement the star quilt and the corners of the painted mirror frame.

ecorator Touches

Corrugated Cardboard Stamping

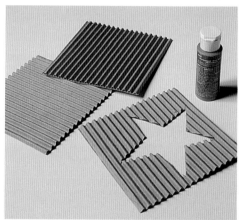

Stars are cut from a square of corrugated cardboard, then used to stamp a border.

Materials

Graph paper
Ten 4" x 4" squares of
    corrugated cardboard
X-Acto® knife
Stencil paint in 2 contrasting colors
2 disposable aluminum pie pans

Directions

1. Measure the area to be painted. On graph paper, calculate the number of repeats for each 4" x 4" stamped square and the amount of space between squares. In the photo above, plain squares were stamped in varying directions on the lower portion of the wall, then the cutout squares were stamped in a contrasting color as a border.

2. Draw 3 different star shapes. Using an X-Acto knife, cut each star from the center of a 4" cardboard square. Leave the remaining squares uncut.

3. Pour one color of the stencil paint into a pie pan. Use the uncut squares to stamp the lower portion of the wall. Dip a square into the paint and press the excess paint onto a piece of paper. Stamp 3 to 4 times per paint application, rotating the stamp so the lines run in both directions. When the lines blur, start a new piece of cardboard.

4. Use the contrasting paint and the star squares to stamp a border, alternating the stars and the direction of the lines.

Above: A garden theme brightens a bathroom in the home of Kathy and David Renzelman. Kathy stenciled the shower curtain, then added accents of ivy, twig baskets, and silk flowers.

The dressing area of Joan and Jim Hanson's master bath is filled with personal touches. A small Basket quilt hangs on the far wall. China, silver, and other collectibles that once belonged to Joan's mother add a touch of charm.

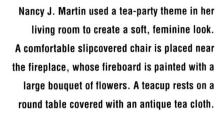

Nancy J. Martin used a tea-party theme in her living room to create a soft, feminine look. A comfortable slipcovered chair is placed near the fireplace, whose fireboard is painted with a large bouquet of flowers. A teacup rests on a round table covered with an antique tea cloth.

*Home is where
the heart is.*
—PLINY THE ELDER

Decorations on a Theme

*T*he easiest way to decorate a room is to pick a theme. Themes can be hobbies, collections, sports, or characters from films and literature. The possibilities are limitless!

The architecture of a building can suggest a theme, especially in the case of converted barns, churches, or public buildings. Vacation homes are often decorated by theme, such as lodge, nautical, or sports motifs.

Theme decorating is a great way to tie a room together. The theme often suggests a color scheme, such as a red-white-and-blue Americana or a delicate pastel tea party. A theme can also suggest a style of furniture or be a great source of ideas for charming and unusual accents, art, and collectibles.

Left and below:
At Christmastime,
diminutive Santas
from Nancy's
collection join the
party on the mantel.

Above: A small tree decorated with tea items
appears during the holidays in a corner of the room.

Left: The focal point of the room is the mantel
grouping above the fireplace. It features a collection
of tea-party needlework, books, and pottery.

Inspired by a visit to Norway, Nancy accented this small apartment with Scandinavian textiles and her collection of blue-and-white dishes. She chose warm red walls to showcase the pine cabinets and ceiling.

Above: In the sleeping alcove are two red-and-white all-American quilts: Pine Tree on the wall and Double Irish Chain on the bed. Sheeting fabric from Norway coordinates with antique pillowcases and a plaid pillow from Holland.

Left: Blue-and-white dishes are displayed on a special shelf above the sliding-glass door. The tab curtains are made from Swedish fabrics. More blue-and-white plates are hung in groupings on the wall.

Above: Bob and Jeanne Bradley's home, a remodeled church in Sutton Mills, New Hampshire, features an open area with the living room in the foreground. The kitchen occupies a raised area at the back, formerly the altar.

Right: Two quilts by Carol Doak, "Victorian Baskets" and "Hearts and Flowers," hang on the back wall. "Dreaming of Spring" by Beth Meek graces the sofa. A miniature quilt rests on the coffee table.

Left: Quilts by Ginny Guaraldi brighten the dining area. The leaded glass windows are original to the church.

Below: By the stairs to the choir loft are a Petite Baskets quilt by Carol Doak (on the wall) and "Rustic Alabama" by Ginny Guaraldi (draped over the grand piano).

Right: A church pew provides seating on one side of the kitchen table. Colorful quilts mix with other collectibles for an interesting wall grouping.

Above: A collection of antiques and collectibles adds interest to this all-white kitchen, as does the "American as Apple Pie" quilt by Beth Meek.

Right: Vintage scrap quilts from the collection of Peggy and Norm Forand brighten this guest room. The quilts tied around the bedposts are from the collection of Jeanne and Bob Bradley.

In the foyer, "Hearts and Flowers" by Carol Doak hangs above an old church pew. A scrap quilt by Moira Clegg and the aptly named "Sunrise Service" by Ginny Guaraldi soften the pew.

The Well-Decorated Office

*W*ith more and more women occupying executive positions in companies or telecommuting from a home office, more attention is being paid to office decor. High-tech office environments with computer terminals and their myriad wires are being softened with cozy quilts, bright fabrics, and personal mementos, creating a relaxed, comfortable setting.

Nancy J. Martin's office at That Patchwork Place provides an atmosphere in which she can not only enjoy her quilts but also conduct business meetings. The challenge was to brighten green cloth walls, hunter green carpet, and a scarred oak floor in the corner. Rather than refinish the floor, Nancy had designer Susan I. Jones paint a patchwork rug in this area.

Wicker chairs with patchwork cushions and a windowsill full of memorabilia from 20 years of business personalizes the office, as does the Rose Wreath quilt on the wall.

Above: In the home office of Terry and Cherry Jarvis of Woodinville, Washington, a sturdy work table holds a computer and printer. Terry stenciled a checkerboard border next to the ceiling to complement the striped fabric of the window valances. Terry's collection of office machinery and mementos from his Vintage Auto Parts business add charm to the room.

Below: Detail of window treatment

Left: Behind the computer table, a vintage brass bed is dressed in a large-scale floral duvet cover and complemented by a tailored bed skirt, pillow shams, and a cozy quilt.

That which is gathered and shared multiplies.

—UNKNOWN

Collections

*C*ollecting isn't just a matter of acquiring objects; it's the thrill of the chase. Most collectors go into antique shops, thrift stores, or yard sales with several different objects in mind. These objects are missing pieces in a category, theme, or color range. My current list includes pink-and-white china, blue-and-white china, brown-and-white Staffordshire plates, red-and-green quilts, teapots and related objects with a tea theme, hunting and fishing items or those with a lodge look, antique sewing notions, pressed flower pictures, birdhouses, twig furniture, and miniature chairs. When I deem a certain collection complete, I add another category to the list.

It takes patience to amass a collection and a discerning eye to display it to maximum advantage. Concentrating collections in a specific area, such as a tabletop or a corner of a room, focuses the display. Containers—such as baskets, hutches, open shelves, peg racks, or display cases—are ideal for displaying smaller objects.

Left: Khay Norris uses a 1940s kitchen cabinet to display culinary collectibles from the same era.

Right: Nancy J. Martin often combines several collections in her decorating schemes. Here, she grouped pink-and-white plates with a sponge-painted mirror above a miniature-chair collection displayed on the table.

Left: Cleo Nollette elevated her teapot collection on a platform covered with black-and-white checks. Miniature quilts by Mary Hickey brighten the background.

Left: Karen Snyder's collection of rolling pins nestles in an antique dough bowl.

Above, top: Christal Carter's Santa mugs spread holiday cheer from a hutch.

Above, bottom: A store display case houses Christal's collection of cookie cutters. A heart collection fills the countertop and shelves.

Christal's collection of log cabins sets up housekeeping in a bookcase.

Above: Karen Snyder's collection of Georgia folk pottery gleams on the mantel. Architectural stars, which Karen also collects, accent the brick fireplace.

Above and left: Tartan plaids and golf paraphernalia make an interesting display in the home of Khay and Don Norris. More tartan collectibles are grouped in the corner.

Left: Inspired by Christal Carter's arrangement (shown on page 71), Nancy J. Martin stacked two vintage suitcases and a wicker bed tray to fashion this impromptu but functional coffee table.

Smaller sewing implements and
tools fill a shadow box.

A 30"-high bookcase, built along the back wall of Nancy J.
Martin's sewing studio, provides both storage and a place
to display antique sewing notions. Baskets hold special
collections of fabric or stitching projects in progress.

Above: A collection of antique needle packets

Toy sewing machines await, ready to stitch.

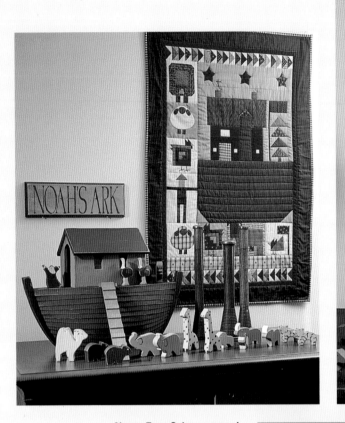

Above: Terry Guizzo arranged her Noah's Ark in front of the Noah's Ark wall hanging designed by Country Threads.

Above, right: Kathy Renzelman's Noah's Ark collection

Right: Nancy J. Martin draped two faded flags across the top of a window to create an unusual valance in this bedroom filled with patriotic accents.

Mary Ghromley's Raggedy Ann and Andy dolls form
a happy crowd in the family room of her home.

Log cabins collected by Christal Carter

Antique sewing items fill a tray on the dressing-room table.

Happiness is homemade.

—UNKNOWN

Sewing Studios

Quiltmakers and seamstresses long for their own space, where they can while away the hours creating fabric masterpieces, then close the door behind them to return another day. This space can be used to design, to stitch, to store fabric and equipment, and to display finished work.

Whether a room of one's own or a corner of the family room, having an area set up and ready to go allows one to stitch at the drop of a pin and not waste precious moments setting up.

Above: In Donna Radner's studio, book-shelves and cubicles hold fabric for future quilts.

Right: Additional shelves and boxes of fabric line the long wall opposite the sewing table.

A cork wall holds a work in progress. The quilt's backing is draped over the ironing board at left.

Quilts and teaching samples are stored in this large cupboard.

When Terry Guizzo built her new home, she designed an 8' x 10' sewing studio off the family room. Kitchen cabinets line the wall and create counter space perfect for rotary cutting. Glass-front cupboards leave Terry's fabrics visible while protecting them from dust, and her birdhouse collection perches happily in the space above.

Decorator Touches

A Patchwork Floor

Materials

Graph paper
Self-adhesive tile flooring in
   contrasting colors
Ruler
Rotary cutter and old blade

Directions

1. Plan the floor design on graph paper.
2. Count the number of quarter-square triangles needed of each color. Divide by 4 to determine the number of tiles to cut.
3. Using a ruler and rotary cutter, cut the tiles diagonally into quarters.
4. Beginning in a corner of the room, lay the first row of tiles, following the manufacturer's directions.
5. Consult your graph paper to complete the floor design.

An Ohio Star quilt design decorates the floor of Terry Guizzo's sewing room.

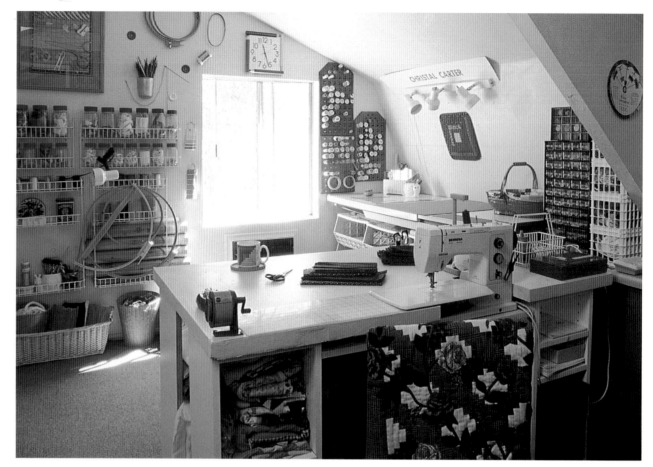

Christal Carter's sewing studio occupies the top floor of a barn built on their property. Her storage system is both functional and decorative.

Below: Recycled instant coffee jars contain assorted sewing notions. The red lids add a splash of color.

Wooden spools of thread and notions are grouped together in a small display case.

Above: Another area holds
a futon couch and a desk.

Left: Art supplies are arranged
in this old wooden display box.

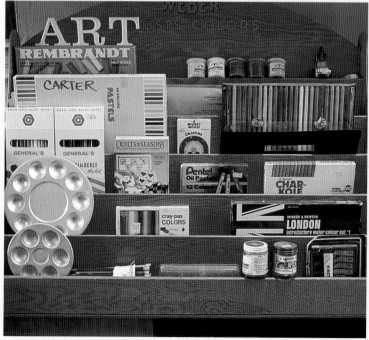

Colored pencils are stored in a basket
hung from a whimsical display piece.

Retta Warehime devoted one end of her family room to sewing and quilt design. The bank of windows makes this a great area to work in, whether Retta is at the machine, the cutting table, or the drafting board.

This novel wooden house is really a filing box, used to hold quilting patterns and designs.

Left: Retta's collection of old and new quilts peeks out from this cabinet inherited from her grandmother.

Below: Seed buckets filled with cuts of plaid fabric hang from a bookshelf.

Above: Joan Hanson uses one leg of her L-shaped family room for quiltmaking and sewing. Antique linens top the curtainless windows, allowing plenty of natural light to enter. Joan positioned her sewing cabinet so she could enjoy the view of the water. A custom-built cutting table allows plenty of room for large projects. The cover quilt from Joan's book *Sensational Settings* hangs on the wall.

Right: The rest of the Hanson's family room is devoted to family activities. There's also space for quilt and fabric storage and a computer work area.

In Nancy J. Martin's sewing room, two sewing cabinets occupy center stage, allowing both Nancy and her assistant, Cleo Nollette, to have separate and easily accessible work areas. Pastel walls, and white sewing cabinetry trimmed with oak contribute to a restful atmosphere.

Two separate cutting tables include wire baskets underneath for fabric storage. Positioned between tall storage units, one cutting surface is just steps away from the machines. A second table (not shown) stands in the center of the room.

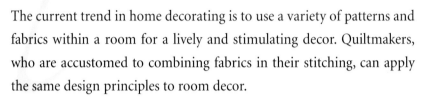

Part 4

Fun with Fabric

The current trend in home decorating is to use a variety of patterns and fabrics within a room for a lively and stimulating decor. Quiltmakers, who are accustomed to combining fabrics in their stitching, can apply the same design principles to room decor.

I prefer to design my rooms around the fabric, choosing the paint and carpet to coordinate. This is fine if you are starting a room from scratch, but often there is existing paint or carpet to work around. Don't be too concerned with matching the colors exactly. They will look different anyway, depending on the light source and reflection at different times of the day. Just be sure to make your color decisions under typical lighting conditions, whether natural or artificial.

The easiest way to mix fabrics in a room is to use a collection that has been designed to be used together. Some of these collections also include wall coverings and bed linens.

When I designed the Room Mates™ collection, my goal was to coordinate a line of fabrics that could be used for home decor *and* quiltmaking. Thus, there are heavier-weight yarn dyes for upholstery, large-scale prints for slipcovers and draperies, 54"-square fabric panels for a variety of uses, stripes for borders, bed skirts, and valances, plus smaller-scale lightweight prints for quiltmaking.

Whether you use a coordinated fabric collection or combine fabrics on your own, it's helpful to keep the following tips in mind:

- Be sure to vary the scale of the fabrics. Too many large-scale prints will compete for attention, while too many tiny prints can be boring.
- Match the scale of the print to the size of the area it will cover. For example, use large-scale prints for sofas or draperies, medium-scale prints for table covers or chair cushions, and smaller prints as accents. Prints that are too small will most likely go unnoticed in a large room.

- Replace solid colors in a decorating scheme with coordinated geometrics, checks, or stripes to add pizzazz.

- Use color or a theme to tie fabrics together. When linking with color, be sure the same tones appear in each of the prints. A theme or novelty motif can further unify the fabrics.

- Don't be afraid to use texture. Textured fabrics, such as nubby linen, bumpy chenille, smooth damask, raw silk, or ribbed corduroy, can add interest to a room. For a serene feel, try using solid beige, taupe, or cream-colored fabrics, relying on texture rather than pattern to set them apart.

Remember, fabric shopping is fun, and the fabric you choose should appeal to you. You'll most likely need to live with your choices for a while, so make sure you are sold on the fabric. You may take a friend or decorator along for advice, but in the end, it's you who will see this fabric on a daily basis, so make sure you like it.

Strategy

Select a fabric that inspires you, then stand back or squint to get an overall impression and determine what color it "reads." Resist the temptation to use a fabric just because it has a few tiny dots of the perfect shade. Also remember not to reject a fabric because it has a speck or two of the *wrong* color. After selecting the main fabric, look for additional fabrics that relate to or contrast with the main fabric.

Overlap swatches of your selections to observe their effect on each other. Seen side by side, fabrics can add or subtract color from each other. Each size of the swatch should reflect the extent to which that fabric will appear in the decor. Do you plan to reupholster a sofa, love seat, and chair with the fabric, or to make a simple 12" x 12" pillow? Once you have decided, buy and work with appropriately sized swatches. Purchase at least ½ yard of the main fabric you are considering. If the fabric doesn't work, don't think of the purchase as a waste of money—it just saved you from buying a huge quantity of a fabric you don't want. This is also true for paint and carpeting. It's extremely difficult to evaluate color using a 2" x 3" paint chip.

In deciding what goes where, consider that printed fabrics have visual weight. Don't cluster "heavy" fabrics, such as dark or large-scale prints, in one area. Balance heavier patterns throughout the room, unless you want to draw attention to a specific area, in which case, make sure there are heavy pieces of furniture or other strong elements elsewhere in the room that will balance this grouping of fabrics. Small-scale prints are easier to work with since they can be integrated into any area of the room without disturbing the proportion or balance.

A variety of patterns and fabrics from the Provence color group of Room Mates™ fabric are combined in this living room.

The Provence color group from the Room Mates fabric collection delights the eye as it brightens the living room. The sofa and love seat were slipcovered patchwork style by Deanna Heathcock of Deann Designs. Square fabric panels are used as table toppers over the floor-length cloth. A Star of Provence quilt hangs on the wall above the sofa with its assortment of coordinating pillows. A slipcovered chair features a pillow from another Room Mates fabric. Simple half-circle window toppers made from the Room Mates striped print add a finishing touch to the windows while allowing light into the room.

In the adjoining dining room, more Provence Room Mates fabrics team up for a stylish eating area. A square fabric panel is hemmed as a tablecloth and matches the mitered-corner napkins. Slipcovers envelop the backs of the ladder-back chairs, and simple tie-on covers adorn the seats. The window seat (left) is covered with a large-scale blue-and-white–check Room Mates fabric and coordinating pillows.

The Kashmir color group from the Room Mates collection has a dramatic decorating impact in this master bedroom. A Shaded Nine Patch quilt hangs on the wall. The bed is dressed in a reversible duvet cover, coordinating pillowcases, flanged pillow shams, and a bed skirt.

Cushions and pillows in the Fairmeadow Room Mates fabrics brighten the porch swing. Be sure to Scotchgard® fabrics used in an outdoor setting.

This bright and cheery bedroom in the home of Kristin and Jon Adams features fabrics from the Fairmeadow color group of Room Mates fabrics. The draped window topper echoes the colors used in the duvet cover, layered bed skirt, and assorted pillows. Two Room Mates fabrics slipcover the apple crates used as nightstands.

The crisp and efficient home
office of Jon Adams is done in
Room Mates Kashmir fabrics.
The window seat (left) is covered
in a perky check, which is
softened with pillows.

Fairmeadow Room Mates fabrics create a soft, restful atmosphere in this guest bedroom. A large-scale print combines with tablecloth panels for the duvet cover. A Medallion quilt hangs above ruffled pillow shams. The slipcovered chair and ruffled pillow add a feminine touch. Additional Room Mates coordinates are used for the bed skirt, tablecloths, pillowcases, and tieback curtains.

The Provence color group from the Room Mates collection is used to brighten this small apartment. Square panels are folded to form a triangular valance. The chairs have been painted to match the tablecloth fabric. The sleeping area features an antique quilt with matching bed skirt and pillowcases.

Tab-top curtains with ties frame the sliding door.

A square tablecloth panel is cut to make a simple gathered valance and cafe curtain.

Three square tablecloth panels are draped to create the nip-and-tuck window treatment.

Helpful Techniques

Matching Pattern Repeats

Print fabrics are not random. They are printed on a roller, and the design repeats over and over along the length of the fabric. A pattern repeat is one complete pattern unit. If you have ever hung wallpaper, you are all too familiar with this concept. On 54"-wide decorator fabric, repeats are generally marked along the selvage edge, and patterns match up along the edge.

Measure the pattern repeat of any fabric you will be joining with lengthwise seams. If you plan to join two panels of fabric, use this measurement and purchase one extra repeat of fabric to allow for matching. If more than two panels are to be pieced together, such as for wide drapes, purchase an extra repeat for each additional panel.

For some items, such as round tablecloths and duvet covers, you don't want a seam running down the center. To avoid this, split the second panel in half lengthwise and sew one half to each side of the main panel along the selvage edge to take advantage of the pattern repeat markings. If you choose a fabric that does not match along the selvage, you will need to cut away fabric along the edges until the motifs match exactly. (Don't forget to take seam allowances into account.) Choosing a pattern with a small repeat results in less waste.

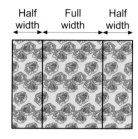

Half width | Full width | Half width

Two panels

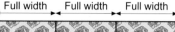

Full width | Full width | Full width

Three panels

Narrow Hems

A neat finish for many decorating projects is a narrow hem. To stitch a narrow hem, first press the raw edge under ¼", wrong sides together. Turn the pressed fabric under a second time and press again. Stitch close to the first folded edge.

Double-Fold Hems

Double-fold hems are used on the side edges of curtain panels and on the lower edges of curtains, bed skirts, and valances. To make a double-fold hem, first turn the raw edge under, wrong sides together, and press. Turn under a second time and press again. Stitch close to the first folded edge.

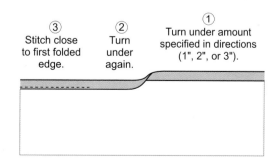

③ Stitch close to first folded edge.　② Turn under again.　① Turn under amount specified in directions (1", 2", or 3").

Covered Cording

Cording inserted in pillows, cushions, or around the edge of floor-length tablecloths gives your decor a finished look. Cording can be purchased in a variety of solid colors, but selection is limited. Homemade cording solves this problem, and it's so easy to make!

Materials

1 yd. of 44"-wide print or solid fabric (yields 750" or almost 21 yards of bias cording)*
Cording

*For ³⁄₁₆"-diameter cording, an 18" x 18" square yields 288" or 8 yds; a 12" x 12" square yields 126" or 3½ yds.

To cover cording:

1. Purchase cording in the desired size. I prefer size 150 (³⁄₁₆" diameter).
2. To determine the width of the bias strip, use a tape measure to measure around cording. Add 1" for seam allowances. For ³⁄₁₆"-diameter cording, cut bias strips 1½" wide.
3. Determine the length needed by measuring the edges to be trimmed and adding 10" to 15" for insurance.
4. Cut strips on the true bias as shown, unless the pattern is not printed on the true bias. In this case, adjust your cutting so the pattern runs down the center of each strip.

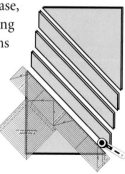

Cutting bias strips with a rotary cutter and Bias Square

5. To join bias strips, place strips right sides together and at right angles, allowing for a ½"-wide seam allowance. Stitch the seam and press open.

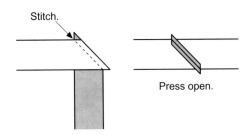

Stitch.

Press open.

6. Fold the bias strip over the cord, wrong sides together and raw edges even. Stitch close to the cord, using a zipper foot. (Special cording or piping feet are available for many machines. For Bernina®, a #12 tricot foot works well with ³⁄₁₆"-diameter cording.)

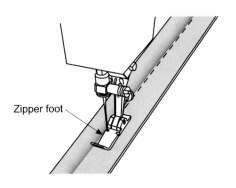

Zipper foot

To attach cording:

1. Never start in the corner of a pillow or cushion. Always begin away from the corners, along a straight edge.
2. Place the cord on the right side of the fabric to be trimmed, raw edges even. Pin around the outside edge.
3. To join the ends, clip the ends of the fabric and cord, leaving a ½" overlap.

Pull one end of the cord out of its fabric casing and trim away ½". Turn under the raw edge of the bias fabric ¼", insert the other end, and slipstitch closed.

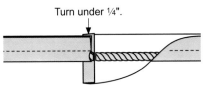

Turn under ¼".

To join cording, trim cord so ends abut.

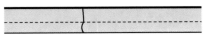

Overlap to cover ends of cord. Stitch.

4. Stitch the cord to the fabric, using a zipper or cording foot. Remove the pins.
5. Place the pillow or cushion pieces right sides together. Keeping the fabric with the cording on top, stitch the pieces together using the previous stitching line as a guide. Sew exactly on this line or slightly inside it to prevent the previous stitching from showing when the fabric is turned. When you reach a corner, use a square turn in the corners for lighter fabrics and a rounded turn for heavier fabrics. Clip the corners as shown.

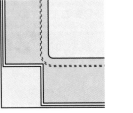

Square turn
for lighter fabrics

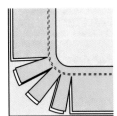

Rounded turn
for heavier fabrics

Bed Linens

Basic Measurements

Standard Mattress

Twin	39" x 75"
Full	54" x 75"
Queen	60" x 80"
King	72" x 84"
California King	78" x 84"

Waterbed Mattress

Single	48" x 84"
Queen	60" x 84"
King	72" x 84"

Daybed Mattress — 39" x 75"

Crib Mattress — 27" x 52"

Bed Pillow

Standard	20" x 26"
Queen	20" x 30"
King	20" x 36"
European	26" x 26"

Bedspread

Twin	81" x 110"
Full	96" x 110"
Queen	102" x 115"
King	114" x 120"
California King	120" x 120"

Note: All sizes include a standard drop of 21".

Bed Skirt

Twin	67" x 89"
Full	82" x 89"
Queen	88" x 94"
King	100" x 98"
California King	106" x 98"

Note: All sizes include a standard drop of 14".

Comforter

Twin	60" x 85"
Full	84" x 90"
Queen	90" x 90"
King	106" x 98"

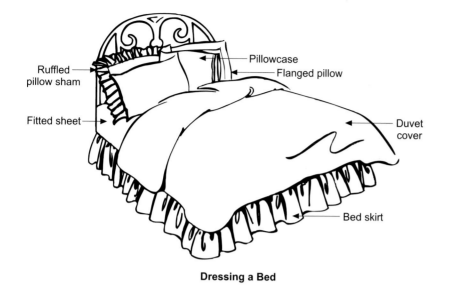

Dressing a Bed

Labels on diagram: Ruffled pillow sham, Pillowcase, Flanged pillow, Fitted sheet, Duvet cover, Bed skirt

Basic Duvet Cover
Color photo on page 194.

A duvet cover is like a giant pillowcase you slip over a down- or polyester-filled comforter. For a proper fit, the cover should be the same size as the comforter. Since comforters vary in size, double-check yours and adjust the dimensions and fabric requirements below if necessary. Creative options include a contrasting panel with button closures and a cover made from tablecloth panels (pages 202 and 203).

Materials

Size	Twin	Full	Queen	King
44"-wide fabric		Yards		
Main fabric	5	5¼	7¾	8½
Lining and ties	5	6¼	7¾	8½
Length of covered cording	240"	275"	280"	310"
54"-wide fabric		Yards		
Main fabric	5	5¼	5¼	8½
Lining and ties	5	5¼	5¼	6
Length of covered cording	240"	275"	280"	310"

Directions

1. Using the measurements given below, cut and piece the main fabric for the duvet top. Be sure to cut extra for matching the pattern repeat (page 199).

Duvet Sizes

Twin	61" x 86"
Full	85" x 91"
Queen	91" x 91"
King	107" x 99"

Second length of fabric is split lengthwise, then matched along selvage edges.

Cut length of fabric.

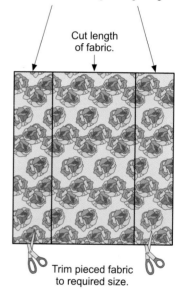

Trim pieced fabric to required size.

2. Cut and piece fabric for the duvet lining, following the directions in step 1.
3. Make covered cording and stitch to the side and bottom edges of the duvet top, following the directions on pages 199–200.
4. Place the duvet top and the lining right sides together. Pin, then stitch the side and lower edges with a ½"-wide seam allowance, using the cording stitching line as a guide. Sew on or just inside this line so previous stitching will not show. Clip the corners and turn right side out.

5. To make ties:
   a. From the lining fabric, cut 12 pieces, each 4" x 14".
   b. Fold each tie in half lengthwise, right sides together. Stitch along the long edge and one short edge, using a ½"-wide seam allowance and leaving one end open.
   c. Clip the corners and turn right side out. Press.
6. Pin 6 ties along the top edge of the duvet top and 6 ties along the top edge of the lining, raw edges even. Space the ties evenly and match each tie with the corresponding tie on the opposite fabric. Baste in place.
7. From the leftover lining fabric, cut and piece a facing according to the following chart:

Facing Sizes

Twin	4" x 121"
Full	4" x 169"
Queen	4" x 181"
King	4" x 213"

8. Join the ends with a ½"-wide seam allowance to make a continuous strip. Stitch a narrow hem on one edge.
9. Pin the facing to the duvet cover, right sides together and raw edges even. Stitch, using a ½"-wide seam allowance and catching the tie ends.

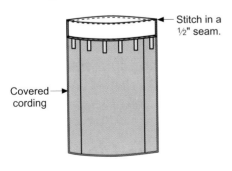

Stitch in a ½" seam.

Covered cording

Duvet Cover with Contrasting Panel and Button Closure
Color photo on page 195.

Materials

Size	Twin	Full	Queen	King
44"-wide fabric		Yards		
Main fabric	5	5¼	7¾	8½
Lining	4¾	5	7¼	8
Contrasting	⅞	⅞	1¼	1¼

Covered cording: Add 1 duvet width to the lengths on the previous page.

Size to Piece

Size	Twin	Full	Queen	King
Lining	61" x 80¼"	85" x 85¼"	91" x 85¼"	107" x 93¼"
Contrasting	61" x 12¼"	85" x 12¼"	91" x 12¼"	107" x 12¼"

Directions
1. Cut and piece the main fabric for duvet top as indicated in step 1 on page 201.
2. Cut and piece the lining and contrasting panel, referring to the chart above. Be sure to cut extra to match the pattern repeat (page 199).
3. Press under ¼" along the width of the lining and contrasting panel. Press under 2" on each to form a wide hem. Stitch the hems close to the first folded edges.

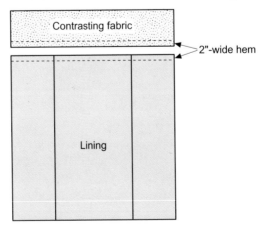

Contrasting fabric

2"-wide hem

Lining

10. Turn the facing to the inside. Press. Slip the comforter inside the cover and tie the ends to secure.

4. Mark 6 evenly spaced buttonholes on the hem of the contrasting fabric. Stitch buttonholes and cut open.
5. Overlap the contrasting fabric onto the lining fabric and mark the button placement under the corresponding buttonholes. Stitch the buttons in place and button, leaving several buttons open so the duvet cover can be turned right side out after stitching. Baste the contrasting panel to the main fabric along the side edges.

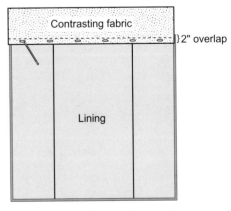

Contrasting fabric

2" overlap

Lining

Mark through for button placement.

6. Make the covered cording and stitch to the edges of the duvet top, following the directions on pages 199–200.

7. Match the lining to the duvet top, right sides together. Pin in place. With the main fabric on top, stitch the pieces together, using a ½"-wide seam allowance and following the cording stitching as a guide. Sew on or just inside this line so previous stitching does not show. Clip the corners and turn right side out.

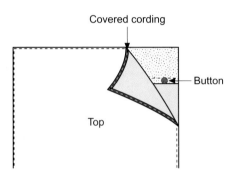

8. Insert the comforter into the duvet cover and button to secure.

Tablecloth Panel Duvet Cover
(not suitable for twin-size bed)
Color photo on page 197.

Materials
Three 54" x 54" tablecloth panels
Contrasting fabric for borders, facing, and ties
Lining fabric (Use yardage requirements for "Main fabric" on page 201.)
Covered cording (Use length given on page 199.)

Directions
1. Trim 1 panel to 54" x 54", spacing the border design evenly on all sides.

2. Cut 2 triangles, each 39" along the short sides, from each of the remaining 2 panels (4 total).

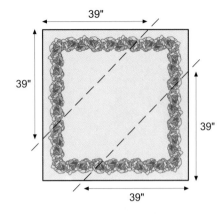

3. Stitch a triangle to each side of the 54" square as shown, using a ½"-wide seam allowance. The resulting square should measure approximately 76" x 76".

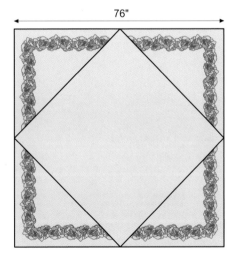

4. Add contrasting borders along the side, top, and bottom edges to build a duvet cover to the size indicated in step 1 on page 201 or to the size of your duvet, if different.

5. Complete the cover, following steps 2–10 on pages 201–202.

Pretty Pillowcases
See "Decorator Touches" on page 155.

Ruffled Pillow Sham
Color photo on page 197.

Materials
For 1 standard-size pillow (20" x 26")
44"-wide fabric: 2⅛ yds.
54"-wide fabric: 2 yds.

Directions
1. Cut a 21" x 27" piece for the pillow front. Cut 2 pieces, each 16" x 21", for the pillow back.

2. To fashion a ruffle with a fullness twice that of the pillow, measure the outside edges of the pillow and multiply by 2 (184").

3. For a 3"-wide finished ruffle, cut and piece 7"-wide strips to achieve the length determined in step 2. Join the short ends to form a continuous strip.

4. Fold the ruffle in half lengthwise, wrong sides together; press. Sew a gathering stitch ⅜" from the raw edges of the ruffle. Gather to the length of the outside edges of the pillow.

5. Pin the gathered ruffle to the pillow front, right sides together and raw edges even. Ease extra fullness into the corners and pin the outer edges so they will not be caught in the stitching.

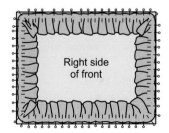

6. Adjust the gathers to fit; baste.

7. Stitch a narrow hem on one 21" edge of each pillow back.

8. Overlap the pillow backs on top of the pillow front, right sides together, as shown. Pin.

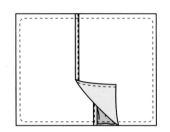

9. Stitch, using a ½"-wide seam allowance. Clip the corners and turn right side out. Insert the pillow form through the opening.

Flanged Pillow Sham
Color photo on page 194.

Materials
For 1 standard-size pillow
(20" x 26")

1½ yds. fabric
3½ yds. covered cording (page 199)

Directions

1. Cut 1 piece, 27" x 33", for the pillow front. Cut 2 pieces, each 20" x 27", for the back.

2. Baste the cording to the pillow front, following the directions on page 200.

3. Stitch a narrow hem on one 27" edge of each pillow back.

4. Overlap the pillow backs on top of the pillow front, right sides together, as shown in the diagram at left.

5. With the pillow front on top, stitch just inside the previous stitching.

6. Turn right side out and press.

7. Topstitch 3" from the finished edge on all sides to form a flange. Insert your pillow form through the opening.

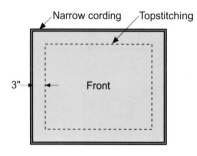

Bed Skirt
Color photo on page 194.

A bed skirt hides the box spring and bed frame. A standard bed skirt has a 14" drop, measured from the top of the box spring to the floor. Adjust the length (and fabric requirements) if your box spring and bed are higher. The platform top of a bed skirt fits between the box spring and mattress. Add split corners to your bed skirt if you have a four-poster bed. A creative option for a layered bed skirt follows the main directions.

Directions

1. Cut and piece the platform fabric to one of the following sizes:

Twin	40" x 76"
Full	55" x 76"
Queen	61" x 81"
King	73" x 85"

2. Stitch a narrow hem on the top edge of the platform fabric.

3. For the skirt, refer to the chart below, then cut 16½"-wide crosswise strips of fabric and piece along the selvages until the desired length is achieved (see chart). Press the seams open.

Materials

Size	Twin	Full	Queen	King
		Yards		
Muslin or other lightweight fabric for platform (44"-wide)	2¼	3⅛	3½	4¾
Skirt fabric*				
44"-wide	5½	6	6½	7
54"-wide	4⅔	4⅔	5⅛	5½
Strong twine	14	14½	15½	16¾

See note on page 205.

Cutting for Skirt

Size	Twin	Full	Queen	King
No. of 16½" strips (44"-wide fabric)	11½	12½	13¼	14½
No. of 16½" strips (54"-wide fabric)	9	10	11	12
Length to piece	480"	518"	558"	608"

Note: If you want your fabric pattern to run parallel to the floor, as with a border print, you must cut lengthwise strips instead. Recalculate the yardage requirements, remembering you will get only two 16½" lengthwise strips from one width of 44"-wide fabric.

4. Hem the lower edge by turning under 1", wrong sides together. Press. Turn under a second time and press again. Stitch close to the first folded edge. Refer to the directions on page 199.

5. Stitch a narrow hem on each end of the skirt.

6. To gather the skirt, lay the twine ⅜" from the raw edge. Zigzag over the twine, being careful not to catch the twine in the stitching. Gently pull the twine to gather. Adjust the fullness.

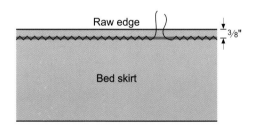

7. Pin the skirt to the platform, right sides together, adjusting the fullness of the skirt. A little extra fullness at the corners will give a lush look.

8. Stitch the skirt to the side and bottom edges of the platform, using a ½"-wide seam allowance.

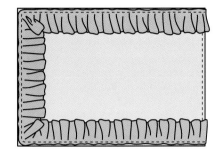

9. Slide the platform of the bed skirt between the box spring and mattress, and allow the skirt to fall gracefully to the floor.

Creative Option:
Layered Bed Skirt
Color photo on page 195.

Add a second skirt for an even more opulent look. For the shorter (top) skirt, cut 12"-wide strips, using the number in the directions above. After hemming, layer the shorter skirt on top of the longer one and gather as a single unit, using the twine as directed in step 6. Assemble the skirt, treating the two layers as a single unit.

Cushions, Pillows & Slipcovers

Box Cushions with Contrasting Cording
Color photo on page 192.

Materials
Fabric
Contrasting covered cording (page 199)
Foam or polyester cushion form
Zipper

Directions
1. Measure the cushion form as shown. (Window-seat cushions may have odd angles.)

Work Sheet for Standard Cushion

For sides, add:

length	_____
+ width	_____
+ width	_____
+1"	_____

Total length of sides = _____
Cut 1 of total length by height +1".
For zipper placket, add:

length	_____
+1"	_____

Length of zipper placket = _____
Cut 2 of length by ½ height +1".

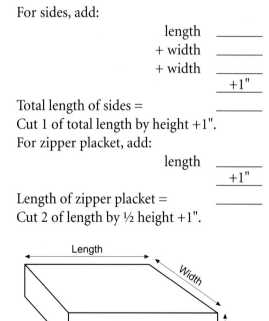

Standard Cushion

Work Sheet for Angular Cushion

For sides, add:

front length	_____
+ width	_____
+ width	_____
	+1"

Total length of sides = _____
Cut 1 of total length by height +1".
For zipper placket, add:

back length	_____
	+1"

Length of zipper placket = _____
Cut 2 of length by ½ height +1".

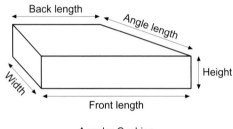

Angular Cushion

2. Referring to your work sheet, cut a piece of fabric for the cushion top and another for the bottom. Cut pieces for the sides and zipper placket.

3. For the zipper placket, place the pieces right sides together and baste along one long edge, using a ¾"-wide seam allowance. Press the seam open. Using a zipper foot, install the zipper as shown.

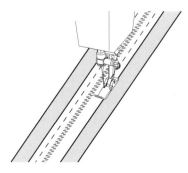

Place zipper face down on inside of seam.
Machine baste in place.

Stitch ⅜" from each side of seam.
Bar tack at each end to stabilize seam.
Carefully remove basting stitches.

4. Stitch the zipper placket to one end of the side. Open the zipper a few inches so the cover can be turned right side out. Remeasure to determine the proper length, then stitch the placket to the opposite end of the side.

5. Stitch contrasting cording to the cushion top and bottom, following the directions on page 200.

6. With right sides together, pin the cushion side to the cushion top. Stitch, using previous stitching as a guide and carefully turning the corners. Stitch again at the corners for reinforcement.

7. Mark the corners on the cushion side, aligning the marks to the cushion-top corners. Pin the cushion bottom to the side, matching corner markings. Stitch, using previous stitching as a guide.

8. Turn the cover right side out through the zipper opening. Insert the cushion form.

Cushions with Tie Ends
Color photo on page 155.

Materials
Main fabric for outer cover and ties
Contrasting fabric for inner cover

Directions

1. Measure the cushion form as shown.

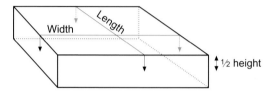

2. Add 1" to the length and width measurements; cut 2 pieces from contrasting fabric for the inner cover.

3. Using the same measurements, cut 2 pieces from the main fabric for the outer cover.

4. Make a facing for the outer cover by cutting away a 3"-wide strip along the width of each main fabric piece.

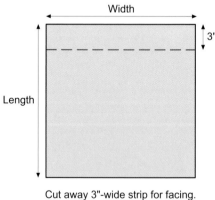

Cut away 3"-wide strip for facing.
Make 2.

5. Cut 6 pieces for ties, each 4" x 14".

6. With right sides together, stitch the inner-cover pieces along 3 sides, using a ½"-wide seam allowance.

7. Tie the sewn corners with twine to soften the edges. Turn right side out and press. Slip over the cushion form.

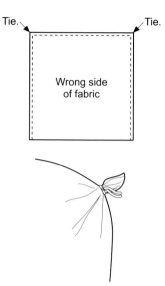

8. To make ties:
   a. Fold ties in half lengthwise, right sides together, and stitch, using a ½"-wide seam allowance and leaving one end open.
   b. Clip the corners and turn right side out. Press.

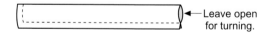

9. Repeat step 6 for the outer cover. Clip the corners and turn right side out.

10. Pin the ties along the top edge of the outer cover, with raw edges even and each pair of ties aligned.

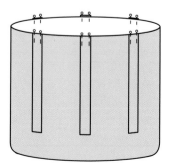

11. With right sides together, stitch the ends of the facing pieces together, using a ½"-wide seam allowance. Stitch a narrow hem on the lower edge.

12. Slip the facing over the outer cover, right sides together, and pin in place. Stitch, using a ½"-wide seam allowance and catching the tie ends.

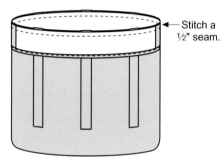

13. Turn the facing to the inside. Press. Slip the cushion form inside the casing, leaving the contrasting fabric exposed. Tie the ends in decorative bows.

Ruffled Pillow
Color photo on page 195.

Materials
Fabric for pillow front, lapped back, and ruffle (See chart at right.)
Purchased pillow form

Yardage for Various Pillow Sizes
(front and back)

Pillow Size	Yards	
	44"-wide	*54"-wide*
12" x 12"	½	½
14" x 14"	½	½
16" x 16"	½	½
18" x 18"	⅝	⅝
20" x 20"	1	⅝
26" x 26"	1¼	¾
30" x 30"	1⅞	1½

Yardage for 3" Ruffles
(three-times fullness)

Form Size	Yards	
	44"-wide	*54" wide*
12" x 12"	⅞	¾
14" x 14"	⅞	¾
16" x 16"	1⅛	⅞
18" x 18"	1¼	⅞
20" x 20"	1¼	1⅛
26" x 26"	1⅝	1¼
30" x 30"	1⅞	1½

Directions
1. For the pillow front, add 1" to the width and length of your pillow form and cut a piece to these dimensions.
2. Cut 2 pieces for the pillow back, using the following equation as a guide:

Pillow size (12") ÷ 2 = (6") + 2" = length of back pieces (8")

Pillow size (12") + 1" = width of back pieces (13")

3. Stitch a narrow hem on 1 long edge of each pillow-back piece.
4. To fashion a ruffle with a fullness 3 times that of the pillow, measure the outside edges of the pillow and multiply this dimension by 3.
5. For a 3"-wide finished ruffle, cut crosswise strips 7" wide and join the short ends to achieve the length determined in step 4.
6. Fold the ruffle in half lengthwise, wrong sides together, and press. Sew a gathering stitch ⅜" from the raw edges. Gather to length of outside edge of pillow.
7. Pin the gathered ruffle to the pillow front, right sides together and raw edges even. Ease extra fullness into the corners and pin the outer edges so they will not be caught in the stitching.
8. Adjust the gathers to fit; baste.
9. Place the pillow backs on the pillow front, right sides together, overlapping as shown in the illustration on page 204 (step 8). Pin.
10. Turn over so the pillow front is on top; stitch the front to the backs. Turn right side out; press. Insert the pillow form.

Button-Trimmed Pillow
Color photo on page 194.

Materials
For one 14" x 14" pillow
½ yd. fabric for pillow front and back
⅜ yd. contrasting fabric for flap
3 buttons, l" to l½" diameter
14" x 14" pillow form

Directions
1. Cut a 15" x 15" piece for the pillow back. From the same fabric, cut a 10" x 15" piece for the pillow front.
2. From the contrasting fabric, cut 2 pieces, each 7" x 15", for the flap.
3. With right sides together, stitch the flap pieces together along one 15" edge, using a ½"-wide seam allowance. Turn right side out and press.
4. Evenly space, then stitch 3 buttonholes onto the flap, close to the finished edge.
5. Stitch a narrow hem along one 15" edge of the pillow front.
6. With right sides together, layer the flap, then the pillow front on top of the pillow back as shown. Pin.

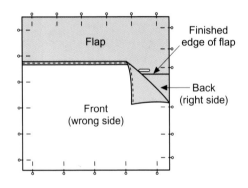

7. Stitch the pillow front and flap to the pillow back, using a ½"-wide seam allowance.
8. Clip the corners and turn right side out.
9. Make placement marks for buttons, then sew to front. Insert pillow form, and button to close.

Tied-Top Pillow
Color photo on page 194.

Materials
For one 16" x 16" pillow
¾ yd. main fabric for outer cover, facing, and ties
⅜ yd. contrasting fabric for inner cover
16" x 16" pillow form

Directions
1. Cut 2 pieces of contrasting fabric, each 10" x 17", for the inner cover.
2. Referring to the diagram below, cut the main fabric for the outer cover, facing, and ties.

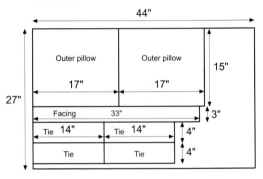

3. With right sides together, stitch inner cover pieces along 3 sides, using a ½"-wide seam allowance.

4. Hem the raw edge of the inner cover. Clip the corners and turn right side out. Press. Slip over the pillow form.
5. To make ties:
   a. Fold each tie in half lengthwise, right sides together. Stitch along the long edge and one short edge, using a ½"-wide seam allowance and leaving one end open.

b. Clip the corners and turn right side out. Press.

6. With right sides together, stitch the outer cover pieces along 3 sides, using a ½"-wide seam allowance. Turn right side out.

7. With right sides together, stitch the short ends of the facing piece to each other, using a ½"-wide seam allowance. Stitch a narrow hem on the lower edge.

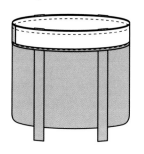

Stitch side in ½" seam.

Narrow hem

8. With right sides together, pin 2 ties along the top edge of each side of the outer cover, raw edges even, making sure placement corresponds with the ties on the opposite side. Pin.

9. Slip the facing over the outer cover, right sides together and raw edges even. Pin. Stitch, using a ½"-wide seam allowance and catching the tie ends.

10. Press the facing to the inside. Slip the pillow form inside the casing, leaving the contrasting fabric exposed. Tie the ends in decorative bows.

Ladder-back Chair Covers
Color photo on page 193.

Materials
For 1 chair cover
(44"- or 54"-wide fabric)
½ yd. main fabric
½ yd. lining fabric
Pattern paper, such as kraft paper
  or newspaper
Small scrap of fusible web

Directions

1. Place the paper on the floor. Place the chair back on top of the paper and trace around the chair back. Add a ½"-wide seam allowance for the top and side edges. The bottom edge should echo the curve of the top edge. Add ¾" to the bottom edge for the hem.

2. Using the pattern as a guide, cut 2 pieces from the main fabric and 2 pieces from the lining fabric. Baste each lining piece to a main piece, wrong sides together, and treat as a single unit.

3. Overcast the top and bottom edges.

4. With right sides together, join the main-fabric pieces along the side edges, using a ½"-wide seam allowance. Stitch the upper edge, leaving a 3"-wide opening at each end for the posts. Backstitch to reinforce.

5. Apply a ¼"-wide strip of fusible web to the upper edge of the lining around the post openings. Do not remove the paper backing.

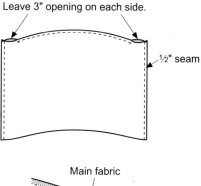

Leave 3" opening on each side.

½" seam

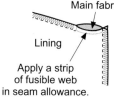

Main fabric

Lining

Apply a strip of fusible web in seam allowance.

6. Turn and press. Peel the backing from the web and carefully fuse the seam allowances around the openings.

7. Turn under ¾" along the lower edge and press, being careful to maintain the curve. Stitch in place close to the overcast edge.

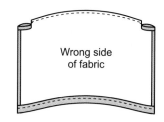

Wrong side of fabric

8. Slip the cover over the back of your ladder-back chair.

Slipcovered Chair
Color photo on page 197.

Choose a kitchen-type chair with a high back and no arms.

Materials

1½ yds. main fabric for chair back, seat, and top skirt
1½ yds. contrasting fabric for bow and long skirt
Covered cording (page 199)
Pattern paper, such as kraft paper or newspaper
Staple gun and staples

Directions

1. Remove the chair seat by removing the screws that hold it in place.
2. Trace paper patterns of the chair back and seat, adding a ½"-wide seam allowance all around and 4" to the length of the chair back.

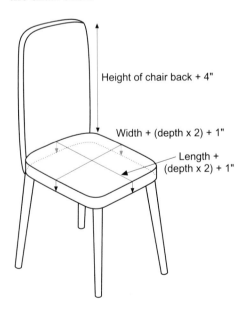

Height of chair back + 4"

Width + (depth x 2) + 1"

Length + (depth x 2) + 1"

3. Cut 2 pieces of fabric for the chair back using the paper pattern. Apply the cording, following the directions on page 200. With right sides together, stitch the chair-back pieces together along the top and side edges. Sew just inside the previous stitching.

Note: Taper the width of the cording so it disappears at a point below the seat.

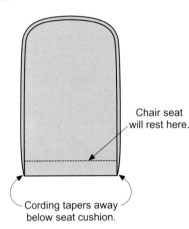

Chair seat will rest here.

Cording tapers away below seat cushion.

4. Slip the fabric over the chair back, turn the chair over, and staple the cover securely in place.
5. Cut 1 piece of fabric for the chair seat.
6. Staple the fabric to the underside of the seat, folding the excess at corners. Place the seat on the chair, but do not screw it in place yet.
7. Cut the fabric for the double skirt according to these measurements:

Long skirt:
Length = distance from bottom of seat to floor + 2" for double-fold hem
Width = Circumference of chair x 2 for gathering

Top skirt:
Length = 8"
Width = Circumference of chair + 48" for corner pleats

8. Stitch a 1" double-fold hem along the bottom edge of the short skirt. Fold in box pleats at each corner as shown.

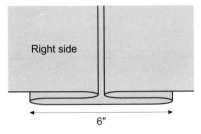

Right side

6"

9. Stitch a 1" double-fold hem along the bottom edge of the long skirt. Gather the top edge to fit the chair seat.
10. Layer both skirts over the chair legs and arrange the short skirt so the pleats fall in the corners. Staple both skirts as a unit to the underside of the seat.
11. Reattach the seat to the chair.
12. A large bow is tacked to the chair back as trim. To make the bow:
    a. Cut 2 pieces of contrasting fabric, each approximately 6½" x 67", tapering the ends.
    b. With right sides facing, stitch the pieces together, using a ¼"-wide seam allowance and leaving an opening for turning. Turn the bow right side out and stitch the opening closed.
    c. Tie into a bow, and tack the loops and knot to the back of the chair.

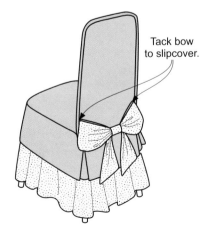

Tack bow to slipcover.

Table Linens

Round Table Skirt

Color photo on page 191.

Materials

Fabric as specified in the chart or determined by the work sheet

Yardstick compass

Work Sheet

If your table size varies from the chart at right, use this work sheet to determine how much fabric you will need:

1. Measure the diameter of your table.

2. Measure the drop. _____

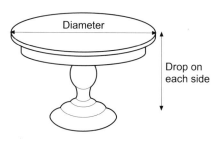

3. Add drop for second side. _____

4. Add the diameter plus the 2 drop lengths plus 1" for hem. This is your fabric cut length. Multiply by 2 if the cut length is greater than the usable fabric width (42" for 44"-wide fabric, or 54" for 54"-wide fabric). _____   +1"

5. Divide by 36" to get the total yards needed. _____

Directions

1. Measure the length of the tablecloth on the fabric and mark. Figure out where you need to start the next cut in order to match pattern repeats. Cut out the 2 panels. Divide the second panel of fabric lengthwise and stitch one half to each side of the first panel, matching the pattern repeats along the seams.

Yardage and Trim for a Round Tablecloth

Table Diameter	Yardage for a 10" drop		Trim Amount for a 10" drop	Yardage for a 30" drop	Trim Amount for a 30" drop
	44"-wide	*54"-wide*	*44"- or 54"-wide*		
30"	2⅞	1½	4½	5	8
36"	3¼	3¼	5	5½	8½
48"	4	4	6	6	9½
54"	4¼	4¼	6½	9½	10
60"	4½	4½	7	10	10½
66"	5	5	7½	10½	11
72"	7¾	5¼	8	11	11½

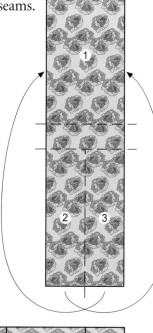

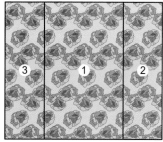

Be sure to match the pattern repeat.

2. Fold the fabric into quarters. Pin the layers together so the fabric does not slip. Using the yardstick compass, place the pivot point at the folded corner. Set the marking end of the compass to measure half the cut diameter. Swing the compass and mark the fabric.

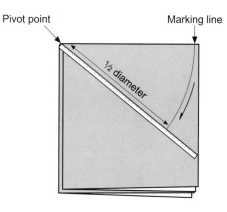

3. Cut fabric along marked line.

4. Finish the raw edges with a narrow hem.

Table Topper
Color photo on page 191.

Preprinted fabric panels add a splash of color to the room decor when layered over floor-length cloths.

Materials
Preprinted fabric panel

Directions
1. Cut the panel so it is square and the motif is evenly spaced on all sides.
2. Finish the raw edges with a narrow hem.

Napkins with Mitered Corners
Color photo on page 193.

Materials
For four 17½" napkins
⅞ yd. main fabric for napkins
⅝ yd. contrasting fabric for trim
Waterproof marking pen or pencil

Directions
1. From the main fabric, cut 4 squares, each 15" x 15", for the napkins.
2. Cut eight 4"-wide strips from the contrasting fabric for the trim. For each napkin, stitch 2 strips together along the narrow ends.
3. Pin the trim to the main fabric along one side of the napkin, right sides together. Starting 1½" from the end of the trim, 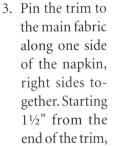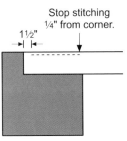 stitch the trim to the napkin, using a ¼"-seam allowance and stopping ¼" from the corner.

4. With a waterproof marking pen, mark a dot on the trim ¼" from the edge of the napkin and ¼" from the bottom of the trim as shown. Draw a straight line between the dot and the point where you stopped stitching.

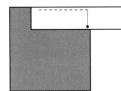

5. Using this line as the measurement, draw a square, then draw an **X** inside the square.

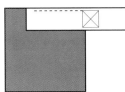

6. Flip under and fold the trim through the center of the **X**, right sides together.

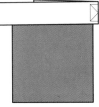

7. Stitch on the diagonal lines, beginning at previous stitching and ending at the marked dot.

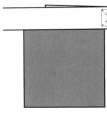

8. Trim the corners ¼" from the stitching; press the seam allowance open.
9. Turn the trim and stitch along the adjacent side, stopping ¼" from the corner.
10. Repeat steps 4–9 to make the remaining mitered corners.
11. On the last side of the napkin, measure the trim, then join the ends of the trim together, using a ¼"-wide seam allowance; press the seam open. Finish stitching the trim to the fabric.

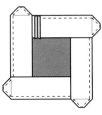

12. Fold trim with right sides together, then turn the raw edges of the trim under ¼", to form a hem. Press.

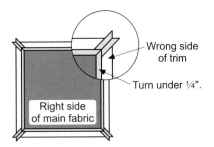

13. Turn the trim right side out and fold it to the wrong side of the napkin. Stitch the edge of the trim to the napkin by hand or machine.

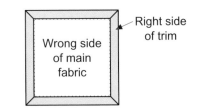

Window Treatments

It's easy to make window treatments that coordinate with the rest of your room. Many of the ideas presented here are time-savers. The window toppers and valances are the easiest to construct, require the least fabric, and allow a lot of light into the room. Creative ideas such as the folded fabric panels or tablecloths and the nip-and-tuck window treatment require little or no sewing.

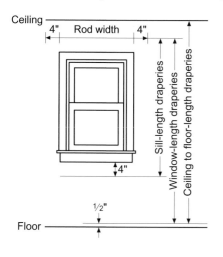

Measurements

Keep the following tips in mind when measuring windows:

- Install hardware first, then take your measurements.
- Use a metal tape measure for window frames and a cloth tape measure for draped swags.
- Measure each window separately. Don't assume all windows in a room are the same size.
- For a plain curtain rod, measure from the top edge of the rod to the point you want the draperies to end for the finished length.

- If using a decorator rod, measure from the eye of the ring to the point you want the draperies to end for the finished length.
- Use the work sheets provided to record measurements and complete cutting lengths.
- Floor-length draperies should come within ½" of the carpeting or floor. Sheers installed under draperies should be 1" shorter than the draperies.

Folded Fabric Panels or Tablecloths
Color photo on page 198.

This is an easy and effective way to dress windows and requires minimal sewing (none at all if you use finished tablecloths). You needn't go to the expense and trouble of installing decorative rods; simply use two push pins to hold the fabric at the corners of the window. Extra fabric will drape gracefully at each corner. I love this technique, because changing the windows is as easy as changing the tablecloths.

Materials

Square fabric panel or tablecloth
Push pins

Directions

1. If using a square fabric panel, cut it so there's an even amount of border on all sides.
2. Stitch a narrow hem on all the raw edges.
3. Fold the tablecloth or hemmed panel diagonally and secure at the corners of the window with push pins. Drape extra fabric to fall gracefully to the front corners.

Half-Circle Window Toppers
Color photo on page 191.

These window toppers are really decorative valances and are quite easy to make. You need only measure the width of the window. Window toppers look best on a 30"- to 40"-wide window. On wider windows, use the same measurements and make two window toppers. It's easy to vary this design by adding a ruffle at the bottom or decorative bows at the corners. Or center the gathering line to create a bustle effect.

Materials
44"- or 54"-wide fabric

2 yds. main fabric
2 yds. lining fabric
1⅛ yds. fabric for contrasting ruffle (optional)
1¼ yds. fabric for pair of decorative bows (optional)
Yardstick compass

Directions

1. Press the main fabric to remove all creases and folds. Fold the fabric in half *crosswise*, making sure the selvages are even.

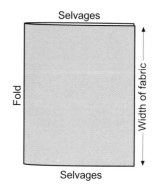

2. Using a yardstick compass, place the pivot in one folded corner and swing the compass to mark a 35" arc.

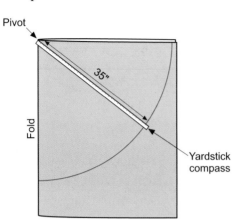

3. Cut along this line. When the fabric is opened, you will have a half circle.
4. Repeat for the lining fabric.
5. If adding the optional ruffle, see below. Otherwise, skip to step 6.
   a. Cut 4 crosswise strips, each 9" wide.
   b. Seam the strips together to make 1 continuous strip.
   c. Fold the strip in half lengthwise, right sides together, and stitch the ends together, using a ½"-wide seam allowance. Clip the corners, turn right side out, and press.
   d. Sew a gathering stitch ⅜" from raw edges. Gather to fit.
   e. Stitch the ruffle to the straight edge of the main fabric as shown, leaving a 4½" unstitched area at each end.

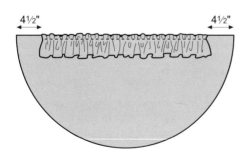

6. On the wrong side of the main fabric, transfer the markings as shown.

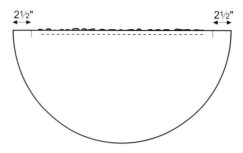

7. Place the main fabric on the lining, right sides together. Pin, being careful not to catch the ruffle. Stitch with a ½"-wide seam allowance, using the ruffle stitching line as a guide. Stitch on this line or slightly inside of it so the previous stitching does not show. Be sure to leave unstitched the opening for turning and the areas marked.

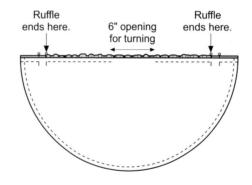

8. Turn the topper right side out and press. Stitch the opening closed.
9. Using the yardstick compass, lightly mark stitching lines for the rod pocket on the lining fabric as shown. Pin the layers together and stitch along the marked lines, backstitching at each end for added strength.

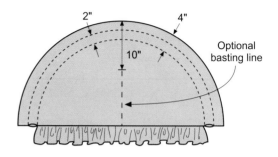

10. Thread the rod through the rod pocket to create a shirred edge.
11. To create a bustle effect, add a basting line in the center of each window topper as shown above. Use a hand sewing needle and 2 strands of thread with the ends firmly knotted together. Stitch a long running stitch from the edge of the window topper or optional ruffle to a point 10" from the curved edge. Draw up the thread to gently gather, then securely knot.

Nip-and-Tuck Window Treatment
Color photo on page 198.

A quick and easy window idea made from tablecloth panels.

Materials
Wooden drapery rods
Assorted tablecloth panels (vintage or new)
String-covered elastic hair bands
Coordinating grosgrain ribbon (optional)

Directions

1. Install the wooden drapery rod.
2. For the side panels, nip one side of each tablecloth panel into an elastic hair band.

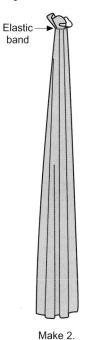

Elastic band

Make 2.

3. Slip a side panel over each end of the rod, using the elastic band to secure the tablecloth to the rod.

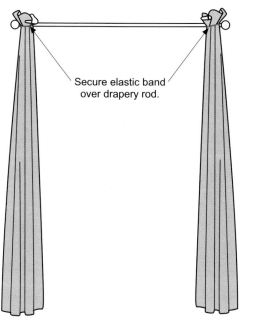

Secure elastic band over drapery rod.

4. For a swag, fold a tablecloth in half and nip the short ends into the elastic bands. (For a wider swag, fold diagonally and nip the corners.) Drape loosely over the rod and tuck the ends inside the elastic bands, securing the side panels.

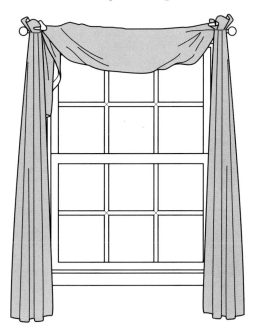

5. Optional: Tie grosgrain ribbon into bows to cover the elastic bands.

Tab-Top Curtains with Ties

Color photo on page 198.

Materials

Decorative curtain rod
Fabric (use work sheet to determine amount)
Fabric scraps for ties

Work Sheet

Width

1. Measure the width of the rod. _____
2. Multiply by 2.5 (or by 3 if more fullness is desired).
   x 2.5 _____
3. Add 4" (for two 1" double-fold side hems). +4" _____
4. Divide by the usable fabric width: 42" or 54". _____
5. Round up to nearest whole number for number of full-width panels. _____
6. Divide by 2 to get the number of panels on each half of the window. _____

Length

1. Measure from the *bottom of the rod* to the desired length. _____
2. Add 2" for 1" double-fold hem. _____
3. Add 4" for 2" double-fold hem. _____

To calculate the total yardage required, multiply the length of each panel by the total number of panels above. Buy extra fabric to match the pattern repeats if necessary (page 199).

Directions

1. Mount the rod above the window so the ties will be above the window. This ensures there won't be any gaps that allow light to enter.
2. Measure the window and use the work sheet to determine the number of panels to cut. If each side of the window needs 1½ or 2½ panels, cut 1 panel in half lengthwise.
3. Seam the panels together along the selvage edges, using a ½"-wide seam allowance and matching the pattern repeats, if any.

215

4. Stitch 1" double-fold hems (page 199) along each side, being careful not to stretch the fabric.

5. Stitch a 1" double-fold hem along the top edge.

6. Repeat for the second curtain.

7. Cut several strips of fabric, each 1" x 10".

8. Tie pairs of strips around the rod, allowing the lower edges to hang free.

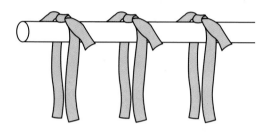

9. Pin the curtain panel to the lower edges of the tied tabs to determine spacing and length. Space tabs from 3" to 8" apart. Mark the location of each pair of tabs along the top of the curtain.

10. When you're happy with the way the top edge looks, measure the curtain from the top to where you want the lower edge to fall. Pin-mark at several places. Remove the curtain by untying the tabs.

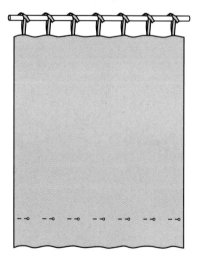

Pin-mark location
of finished bottom edge.

11. Stitch a double-fold hem along the lower edge. For the first fold, bring the raw edge up to the pin markings. Press. Fold again along the pin markings. Press. Stitch close to the first fold.

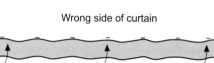

Wrong side of curtain

Fold up until raw edge meets pin marks.

12. From matching or contrasting fabric, cut one 2½" x 20" tab for each location on the curtain panel.

13. Fold the tabs in half lengthwise, right sides together, and stitch ¼" from raw edges, leaving an opening for turning.

14. Turn the tabs right side out and press. Stitch the opening closed.

15. Fold the tabs crosswise and stitch the folded ends to the curtain panel as shown.

16. To install, tie knots or bows around the rod, making sure the curtain falls to the right place. Hang the rod in its brackets.

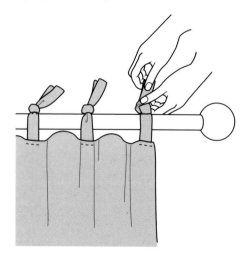

Tieback Curtains
Color photo on page 197.

Materials

Curtain rod
Hooks for tiebacks
2 plastic rings for each tieback
Yardage as calculated on work sheet

Work Sheet

Width

1. Measure the width of the rod and add returns, if any. _____

2. Multiply by 2.5 (or by 3 if more fullness is desired).

   x 2.5 _____

3. Add 4" (for two 1" double-fold side hems). +4"

4. Divide by the usable fabric width: 42" or 54". _____

5. Round up to nearest whole number for the number of full-width panels. _____

6. Divide by 2 for the number of panels on each side of the window. _____

Length

1. Measure from the bottom of the rod to the desired length. _____

2. Add 4" for the top hem. _____

3. Add 4" for a 2" double-fold bottom hem. _____

To calculate the total yardage required, multiply the length of each panel by the total number of panels above. Buy extra fabric to match the pattern repeats if necessary (page 199).

Directions

1. Mount the rod over the window.
2. Measure the window and use the work sheet to determine the number of panels to cut. If each side of the window needs 1½ or 2½ panels, cut 1 panel in half lengthwise.
3. Seam the panels together along the selvage edges, matching the pattern repeats and using a ½"-wide seam allowance.
4. Stitch 1" double-fold hems (page 199) along each side, being careful not to stretch the fabric.
5. Stitch a 2" double-fold hem along the lower edge.
6. Turn under ¼" along the upper edge. Press.
7. Turn under 4" along the upper edge, wrong sides together.
8. Topstitch close to the first folded edge. Stitch again 2" from the first stitching to form a rod pocket.

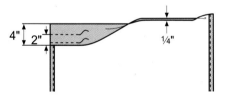

9. To hang the curtains, slip the rod through the rod pocket.
10. To make the tiebacks:
    a. For each tieback, cut a piece of fabric, 9" x 16".
    b. Fold each tieback in half lengthwise, right sides together. Stitch ½" from raw edges, leaving an opening for turning.

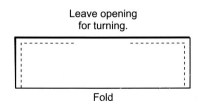

Leave opening for turning.

Fold

c. Clip the corners, turn right side out, and press. Stitch the opening closed.
d. Stitch a small plastic ring to the middle of each end of the tieback.
11. To tie the curtains back, wrap a tieback around each panel and slip the rings over the hooks mounted on each side of the window.

Simple Gathered Valance
Color photo on page 198.

Materials

Curtain rod
Yardage as calculated on work sheet

Work Sheet

Width

1. Measure the width of the rod and add returns, if any. _____
2. Multiply by 2.5 (or by 3 if more fullness is desired).   x 2.5 _____
3. Add 4" (for two 1" double-fold side hems).   +4" _____
4. Divide by the usable fabric width: 42" or 54". _____
5. Round up to nearest whole number for number of full-width panels. _____

Length

1. Measure from the bottom of the rod to the desired length. _____
2. Add 4" for the top hem. _____
3. Add 4" for a 2" double-fold bottom hem. _____

To calculate the total yardage required, multiply the length of each panel by the total number of panels above. Buy extra fabric to match the pattern repeats if necessary (page 199).

Directions

1. Mount the rod over the window.
2. Measure the window and use the work sheet to determine number of panels.
3. Seam panels together along the selvage edges, matching pattern repeats, if any.
4. Stitch 1" double-fold hems along each side, being careful not to stretch fabric.
5. Stitch a 2" double-fold hem along the lower edge.
6. Turn under ¼" along the upper edge. Press.
7. Turn under 4" along the upper edge, wrong sides together.
8. Topstitch close to the first folded edge. Stitch again 2" from the first stitching to form a rod pocket.

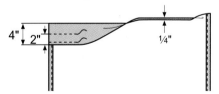

9. Slip the curtain rod through the rod pocket, adjust the fullness, and hang.

Triangular Valance
See "Decorator Touches" on page 152.

Quilts

A quilt is a decorative bed covering consisting of three layers held together by stitching called "quilting." The top layer is decorative and can be pieced or appliquéd. The middle layer consists of batting, and the bottom layer is the backing. Since quilts fall just below the mattress, they are often used with a bed skirt.

The following directions assume some knowledge of basic quiltmaking techniques. The beginner will need to consult one of the introductory quiltmaking books available from That Patchwork Place.

Shaded Nine Patch
Finished Size: 80½" x 80½"
Color photo on page 194.

Nine Patch   Nine Patch   Alternate
Block A   Block B   Block

Fifty 6" Nine Patch blocks and fifty 6" half-square triangle blocks are set in 10 rows of 10 blocks each, with a 10¼"-wide outer border.

Materials
44"-wide fabric

1¼ yds. total assorted light beige prints for Nine Patch blocks

1¼ yds. total assorted burgundy and green prints for Nine Patch blocks

1¼ yds. beige print for half-square triangle blocks

1¼ yds. paisley print for half-square triangle blocks

2½ yds. lengthwise-striped fabric for border (lengthwise pattern must repeat at least 4 times across the width)

5 yds. fabric for backing

¾ yd. fabric for 332" of bias binding

85" x 85" piece of batting

Cutting
All measurements include ¼"-wide seam allowances.

From the assorted light beige prints, cut:
   15 strips, each 2½" x 42", for Nine Patch blocks

From the assorted burgundy and green prints, cut:
   15 strips, each 2½" x 42", for Nine Patch blocks

From the beige print, cut:
   5 strips, each 6⅞" x 42"; cut strips into 25 squares, each 6⅞" x 6⅞"; cut squares once diagonally into 50 half-square triangles for alternate blocks

From the paisley print, cut:
   5 strips, each 6⅞" x 42"; cut strips into 25 squares, each 6⅞" x 6⅞"; cut squares once diagonally into 50 half-square triangles for alternate blocks

From the striped fabric, cut:
   4 lengthwise strips, each 10½" x 86", for border*

Cut strips from identical fabric segments so mitered corners will match.

Directions

1. Join assorted burgundy and green strips and assorted light beige strips as shown to make 5 strip sets. Press the seams toward the darker strips. Crosscut the strip sets into a total of 81 segments, each 2½" wide. Use 62 segments for Block A and 19 segments for Block B.

Burgundy
Light beige
Green

2½"

2. Join assorted light beige strips and assorted burgundy and green strips as shown to make 5 strip sets. Press the seams toward the darker strips. Cut the strip sets into a total of 69 segments, each 2½" wide. Use 31 segments for Block A and 38 segments for Block B.

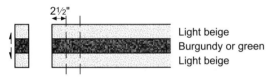

Light beige
Burgundy or green
Light beige

2½"

3. Join the segments as shown to make Block A.

Block A
Make 31.

4. Join the remaining segments to make Block B.

Block B
Make 19.

5. Join the beige print and paisley triangles to make 50 alternate blocks.

Alternate Block
Make 50.

6. Sew the blocks together in 10 rows of 10 blocks each, alternating the Nine Patch blocks and alternate blocks. Refer to the color photograph on page 194.

7. Add the 10½"-wide borders. To miter the corners:

   a. Mark the center of the quilt top on each side. Mark the center of each border on the inner long edge. Stitch the borders to the quilt top with a ¼"-wide seam allowance, matching the centers. The borders should extend beyond the quilt at each end. Start and stop stitching ¼" from the edge of the quilt top. Press the seam allowances toward the border.

   b. Place a corner of the quilt on your ironing board, pinning as necessary to hold it in place. Fold one border under at a 45° angle. Press.

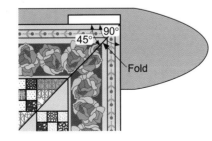

   c. Remove from the ironing board. On the wrong side of the fabric, draw a light pencil line along the crease. Match the border strips, allowing the quilt top to gently fold. Stitch along the drawn line. Check the right side of the fabric to make sure the pattern matches, then trim the seam to ¼" from stitching line. Press seam open.

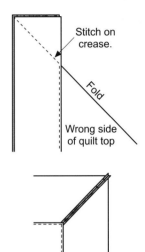

Stitch on crease.

Fold

Wrong side of quilt top

   d. Repeat for the remaining 3 corners.

8. Layer with batting and backing; quilt by hand or machine.

9. Bind with bias binding.

Medallion

Finished Size: 82" x 82"
Color photo on page 197.

Four 14" Basket blocks are used for the center medallion. Five borders surround the center motif: a 2"-wide Sawtooth border, twenty 8" Sawtooth Star blocks, a 3"-wide striped border, forty 6" pieced triangle units, and an 8"-wide floral outer border.

Materials

44"- and 54"-wide fabric

1 fat quarter of light background for Sawtooth border
1 fat quarter of green print for inner Sawtooth border
1½ yds. striped fabric for inner border
2 yds. floral print for outer border
54" x 54" tablecloth panel for Basket blocks
½ yd. each of 9 assorted prints for Sawtooth Stars and triangle border
5 yds. fabric for backing
¾ yd. fabric for 338" of bias binding
86" x 86" piece of batting

Cutting

All measurements include ¼"-wide seam allowances.

From the stripe, cut:
4 lengthwise strips, each 3½" x 54", for 3" border

From the floral print, cut:
8 crosswise strips, each 8¼" x 42", for outer border

From the tablecloth panel, cut:
4 Basket motifs, each 14½" x 14½"

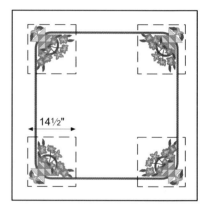

Cut 4.

From the 9 assorted prints and remaining tablecloth fabric, cut a total of:
20 squares, each 4½" x 4½", for centers of Sawtooth Star blocks
80 squares, each 2⅞" x 2⅞"; cut once diagonally into 160 triangles for Sawtooth Star blocks*
80 squares, each 2½" x 2½", for corners of Sawtooth Star blocks*
20 squares, each 5¼" x 5¼"; cut twice diagonally into 80 triangles for Sawtooth Star blocks
40 squares, each 7¼" x 7¼"; cut twice diagonally into 160 triangles for pieced triangle units

To match corners or points, cut in multiples of 4 from each fabric.

Directions

1. Stitch the Basket motifs together to form the center medallion, placing the basket bases toward the corners.
2. To make 60 bias squares for the inner Sawtooth border:
   a. Layer the background and green fat quarters right sides up.
   b. Cut, then piece together 2½"-wide bias strips.

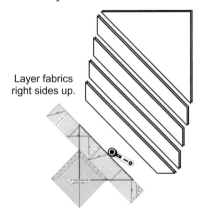

Layer fabrics right sides up.

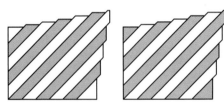

   c. From this pieced fabric, cut 56 bias squares, each 2½" x 2½".

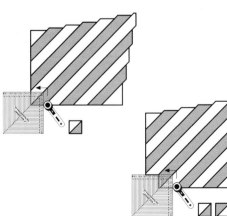

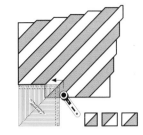

Align 45° mark on seam line and cut first two sides.

Turn cut segments and cut opposite two sides.

3. Join squares to make 4 border strips as shown, each with 14 bias squares.

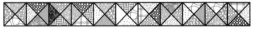

Make 4.

4. Add a background square to each end of 2 of these strips.
5. Stitch the shorter border strips to the sides of the center medallion.
6. Stitch the longer border strips to the top and bottom of the center medallion.
7. Piece 20 Sawtooth Star blocks as shown. Within each block, use the same fabric for all the star tips, and matching fabric for the corners and large triangles.

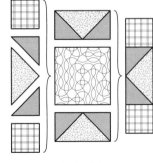

Make 20.

8. Make 2 border strips, each with 4 Sawtooth Star blocks, and 2 border strips, each with 6 Sawtooth Star blocks.
9. Stitch the shorter border strips to the sides of the quilt top.
10. Stitch the longer border strips to the top and bottom of the quilt top.
11. Add the 3½"-wide borders and miter the corners, following the directions in step 7 on page 219.
12. Piece 40 triangle units as shown, mixing and matching a variety of prints in each unit.

Make 40.

13. Make 2 border strips, each with 9 triangle units, and 2 border strips, each with 11 triangle units.

Make 2.

Make 2.

14. Stitch the shorter border strips to the sides of the quilt top.
15. Stitch the longer border strips to the top and bottom of the quilt top.
16. Join two 8¼" floral strips end to end to make a long strip for the outer border. Repeat with the remaining floral strips. Add to the quilt top, mitering the corners as directed in step 7 on page 219.
17. Layer with batting and backing; quilt by hand or machine.
18. Bind with bias binding.

Star of Provence

Finished Size: 84⅛" x 84⅛"
Color photo on page 192.

Star of Provence

Nine 16⅞" pieced blocks are set in 3 rows of 3 blocks each, with 3¼" sashing strips and sashing squares. A lengthwise print makes a neat mitered border.

Materials

44"-wide fabric

3 yds. background fabric
¾ yd. each of 3 different blue prints for feathers and sashing squares
⅝ yd. red print #1 for star tips
1½ yds. red print #2 for sashing
3 yds. lengthwise-striped fabric for border and star centers (lengthwise pattern must repeat at least 4 times across width)
5 yds. fabric for backing
¾ yd. fabric for 346" of bias binding
88" x 88" piece of batting

Cutting

All measurements include
¼"-wide seam allowances.

From the background fabric, cut:
   6 fat quarters, each 18" x 22"
   36 squares, each 2½" x 2½", for Unit 1
   9 squares, each 6⅞" x 6⅞"; cut twice diagonally into 36 triangles for Unit 1
   36 squares, each 2⅜" x 2⅜", for Unit 2
   36 squares, each 4¼" x 4¼", for Unit 2
From each blue print, cut:
   2 fat quarters, each 18" x 22"
   12 squares, each 2⅞" x 2⅞"; cut once diagonally into 24 triangles for Unit 1
From 1 blue print, cut:
   16 squares, each 3¾" x 3¾", for sashing squares
From red print #1, cut:
   36 squares, each 3¾" x 3¾"; cut once diagonally into 72 triangles for Unit 1
From red print #2, cut:
   24 pieces, each 3¾" x 17⅜", for sashing strips
From the stripe, cut:
   9 squares, each 6⅛" x 6⅛", for star centers
   4 strips, each 10½" x 88", for border*

*Cut stripes from identical fabric segments so mitered corners will match.

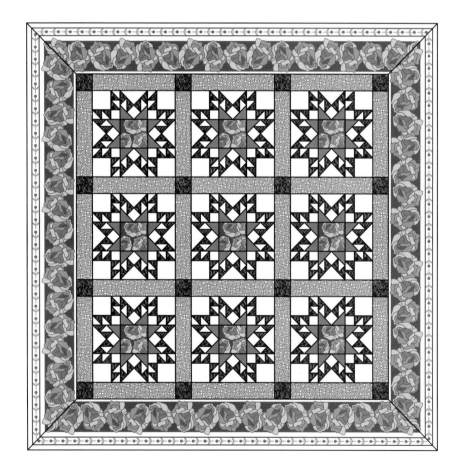

Directions

1. Pair the background and blue fat quarters to make bias squares:
   a. Layer fabrics right sides up.
   b. Cut and piece 2½"-wide bias strips.*
   c. From each blue/background combination, cut 24 bias squares, each 2½" x 2½" for Unit 1 (72 total), and 48 bias squares, each 2⅜" x 2⅜", for Unit 2 (144 total). Keep the different sizes separate.**

2. Piece 36 of Unit 1, using the 2½" bias squares, 2½" background squares, background triangles, blue triangles, and red triangles. Use matching bias squares and blue triangles within each unit.

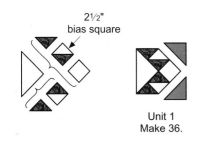

2½"
bias square

Unit 1
Make 36.

3. Piece 36 of Unit 2, using the 2⅜" bias squares and 2⅜" and 4¼" background squares.

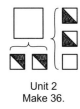

Unit 2
Make 36.

4. Piece 9 Amsterdam Star blocks, using a 6⅛" center square, 4 of Unit 1, and 4 of Unit 2 in each block, matching blue fabrics within each block.

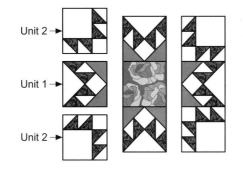

Unit 2 →

Unit 1 →

Unit 2 →

5. Join the blocks into rows, using 3 blocks and 4 sashing strips in each row.

6. Assemble 4 horizontal rows of sashing, using 3 sashing strips and 4 sashing squares in each row.

7. Join rows, referring to the quilt diagram.

8. Add the 10½"-wide borders, mitering the corners as directed in step 7 on page 219.

9. Layer with batting and backing; quilt by hand or machine.

10. Bind with bias binding.

Refer to illustrations in step 2b, page 221.
**Refer to illustrations in step 2c, page 221.*

Publications and Products

 Room Mates™ fabrics are available at all fine quilting and fabric shops.

Many titles are available at your local quilt shop.
For more information, write for a free color catalog to
That Patchwork Place, Inc., PO Box 118, Bothell, WA
98041-0118 USA.

☎ U.S. and Canada, call **1-800-426-3126** for the name
and location of the quilt shop nearest you.
Int'l: 1-206-483-3313   **Fax:** 1-206-486-7596
E-mail: info@patchwork.com
Web: www.patchwork.com   10.96